EXCELLING IN TURBULENT TIMES

How Private Client Lawyers Can Create Exceptional High-Net-Worth Practices in Today's Challenging Environment

RUSS ALAN PRINCE

JOHN J. BOWEN JR.

Excelling in Turbulent Times
How Private Client Lawyers Can Create Exceptional High-Net-Worth Practices in Today's Challenging Environment

By Russ Alan Prince and John J. Bowen Jr.

© Copyright 2017 by AES Nation. All rights reserved.

No part of this publication may be reproduced or retransmitted in any form or by any means, including, but not limited to, electronic, mechanical, photocopying, recording or any information storage retrieval system, without the prior written permission of the publisher. Unauthorized copying may subject violators to criminal penalties as well as liabilities for substantial monetary damages up to $100,000 per infringement, and costs and attorneys' fees.

This book is designed to provide accurate and authoritative information on the subject matter covered. This publication is sold with the understanding that neither the publisher nor the authors provide any assurance as to the correctness or guarantee the accuracy of the contents of the book. Additionally, neither the publisher nor the authors are engaged in rendering legal, medical, accounting, financial, consulting, coaching or other professional service or advice in specific situations. Although prepared by professionals, this publication should not be utilized as a substitute for professional advice in specific situations. If legal, medical, accounting, financial, consulting, coaching or other professional advice is required, the services of the appropriate professional should be sought. Neither the authors nor the publisher may be held liable for any interpretation or misuse of the information in this publication.

The information contained herein is accurate to the best of the publisher's knowledge; however, the publisher can accept no responsibility for the accuracy or completeness of such information or for loss or damage caused by any use thereof.

AES Nation • www.aesnation.com

To Sandi,

There's no one I'd rather grow old and crazy with.

Love, Russ

To all who made it possible:

Private client lawyers who seek to build great lives for their families by making a huge difference.

Our corporate and coaching clients, who taught me what truly works.

My teammates at CEG Worldwide and AES Nation, who brought it all together.

And my wife, Jeanne, and our family, who make it all worthwhile.

– John

Table of Contents

Why You Need This Book 3

PART I

Become Seriously Wealthy 7

Chapter 1 Defining the Private Client Lawyer 9

Chapter 2 Living in Turbulent Times 19

Chapter 3 Building Significant Wealth 31

PART II

In the Line of Money: Today's High-Net-Worth Client Opportunities 41

Chapter 4 The Engine of Private Wealth Creation: Successful Business Owners 43

Chapter 5 The Apex of the Pyramid: The Super Rich and Single-Family Offices 51

Chapter 6 More High-Net-Worth Client Opportunities 61

PART III

Best Practices for Building an Exceptional High-Net-Worth Practice ... 77

Chapter 7 Source Wealthy Clients from Noncompeting Professionals 79

Chapter 8 Benefit from Being a Thought Leader 93

Chapter 9 Maximize High-Net-Worth Client Relationships 105

Chapter 10 Effectively Communicate Legal Strategies 119

Chapter 11 Profit from Value-Based Project Fees 133

CONCLUSION

Building Great Wealth Revisited 145

Why You Need This Book

When we first begin to coach and consult with private client lawyers, we find that most are not enjoying the level of success and building the amount of wealth they want. Given the explosion in both the number of the very wealthy and the amount of wealth they control, they know there are significant opportunities to build exceptional practices serving high-net-worth clients, but they are uncertain about how to tap those openings.

If you are one of the many private client lawyers who wants to build an exceptional practice and be well-rewarded for doing so, we wrote this book for you.

Even as you face turbulent times due to a dramatically and a sometimes adversely changing legal environment, there are still tremendous opportunities for motivated, talented and capable professionals to excel.

In this book, we will delve into the high-net-worth client opportunities and the best practices that can enable you to reach tremendous professional and financial heights—and potentially to become seriously wealthy while doing a remarkable job for your wealthy clients. We will integrate new empirical and ethnographic research on private client lawyers with our deep knowledge of high-net-worth clients. Along the way, we will share hard-learned lessons from other types of elite professionals such as wealth managers, multi-family offices, accountants and the like.

We have two goals with this book:

- To enable you to build an exceptional high-net-worth practice

- To help you profit handsomely by delivering remarkable high-quality solutions to the wealthy

This means delivering outstanding value to wealthy, ultra-wealthy and Super Rich clients. It also means appropriately benefiting financially from delivering high-caliber legal expertise. When you can garner commensurate compensation for the outstanding value you deliver and couple that ability with the astute management of your wealth, it is possible for you to become seriously wealthy.

How do we know what works with the wealthy?

We have had the rare privilege of working directly not only with some of the world's top financial and legal professionals, but with many of the world's wealthiest individuals and families—the so-called Super Rich.

In fact, for a combined total of more than 70 years, we have worked closely with many elite professionals whose practices cater to high-net-worth clients. Their goals are to build relationships with wealthy clients, provide them with the highest caliber services and products available, and ensure an incomparable client experience.

We have also spent decades studying and consulting with the wealthy, including ultra-wealthy business owners, the Super Rich and single-family offices. Our extensive research with these high-net-worth individuals, families and organizations, combined with our "in the trenches" consulting and coaching experiences, has revealed an array of best practices—which we will share with you throughout this book.

In these pages, we define an elite private client lawyer as a legal professional who consistently earns $1 million or more annually. While this is certainly not the norm, we have found it is a very achievable goal, and it will put you squarely on track to amass meaningful personal wealth. Let's get started.

PART I

Become Seriously Wealthy

If you are like most private client lawyers, you want to become wealthier. You probably have several reasons, such as being able to take better financial care of your loved ones and contributing more to charitable causes.

However, you may see yourself constrained by a difficult legal environment that is only likely to become more challenging. From managing greater competition to serving more cost-sensitive wealthy clients, building serious wealth requires a considerable amount of hard, smart work.

At the same time, the tremendous growth in the number of high-net-worth individuals and families and the astounding amounts of wealth they control have made it very possible for you to become a great deal wealthier. The demand for your expertise is sizable and rising.

Achieving significantly greater wealth requires you to strategically concentrate on high-potential, high-net-worth clients. You will need to master and systematically employ empirically validated best practices like the ones we will discuss. If you focus on high-value, high-net-worth clients and put these best practices to work, you will have a strong possibility of building serious wealth.

CHAPTER 1

Defining the Private Client Lawyer

With the astounding boom in private wealth worldwide, your earning potential as a private client lawyer is considerable. This is the case across the entire affluent spectrum, from single-digit millionaires all the way to billionaires.

We see it particularly in two types of potential clients:

- **Successful business owners.** These individuals are creating enormous wealth. In terms of investable assets, three quarters of those with $5 million to $25 million own businesses. Among those with $25 million or more, nine out of ten are business owners. With their increasing wealth and increasing complexity in both their business and personal lives, these individuals need your services and can be the drivers of the success of your practice.

- **Single-family offices.** These offices serving the Super Rich—those with a net worth of $500 million or more—are also growing, both in number and in the amount of monies they control.

As we will discuss, successful business owners, along with single-family offices, are probably the most monetarily appealing types of high-net-worth clients for talented, smart, motivated private client lawyers.

Not all roses and sunshine, but enormous possibilities

Although the number of wealthy individuals and the amount of wealth they control are booming, many private client lawyers conclude that these are very difficult and tumultuous times. The consequence for many is a decreased ability to build solid, let alone exceptional, high-net-worth legal practices, along with the adverse impact this can have on their personal finances and lifestyles.

There are indeed substantial obstacles to your professional and economic success, which we detail in the following chapter. Nevertheless, even in these turbulent times, you can become seriously wealthy as a private client lawyer if you know what to do and commit to acting effectively.

If you recognize and act on the opportunities provided by the growing number and affluence of wealthy individuals and families, you are certainly capable of creating an exceptional high-net-worth legal practice. You can not only play a very prominent role in the legal lives of your wealthy clients, but also very well take center stage amidst the various other professionals, including wealth managers, accountants, bankers and insurance specialists, who serve the moneyed classes. Consequently, if you are knowledgeable and skilled, you can have a significant and positive impact on the lives of your wealthy clients—while financially benefiting along the way.

The private client lawyer

Let's set the stage by defining the private client lawyer.

To determine best practices for private client lawyers, we need to understand exactly the services and expertise they provide. Generally speaking, private client lawyers are specialists in the field of tax and related planning services. For our research and business purposes, their focus is squarely on high-net-worth clients. Thus, we do not consider the services they might provide to institutions, such as private banks that cater to the affluent.

Exhibit 1.1
Private Client Legal Services

The private client lawyer is a professional who provides wealthy clients with these services:

- Planning services, including but not limited to:
  - Estate planning
  - Asset protection planning
  - Income tax planning
  - Succession planning
  - Cross-border and international tax and related planning
  - Business planning for successful business owners
  - Developing charitable giving programs
- Broad-based personal and business advice in which legal considerations are incorporated
- Administrative services tied to the above planning services
- Provisioning of opinion letters and related services such as due diligence on selected tax strategies
- Probate services
- Guardianship and conservatorship services

The private client lawyers who participated in the survey that underpins this book are all practitioners in law firms. Moreover, to meet our definition of a private client lawyer, each professional had to be working for a law firm and provide a specialized set or subset of services to high-net-worth clients (see Exhibit 1.1). The private client lawyers we surveyed also had to derive 80 percent of their income from their legal practices in the service of the wealthy.

Earning a living

Let's assume that all the private client lawyers surveyed—and all high-end professionals, for that matter—have integrity. That is, they are honest and intent on doing the best job possible for their wealthy clients. Keep in mind that both saints and sinners would, in responding to a survey, claim to have integrity. While there are certainly differences in technical proficiencies among private client lawyers and other types of professionals, is it difficult or even impossible to accurately discern these differences in surveys.

In conducting research to determine best practices, differences based on revenues or firm profits pose severe methodological conundrums. Therefore, we typically rely on income differences and variances to differentiate and categorize private client lawyers.

In the survey of 318 private client lawyers, nearly four out of five earn less than $300,000 annually (see Exhibit 1.2). The remaining fifth earn between $300,000 and $600,000 each year.

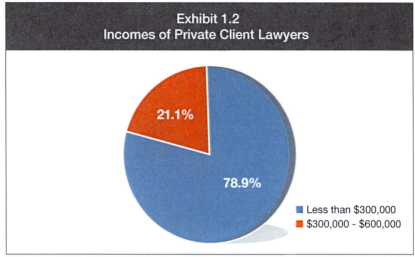

N = 318 private client lawyers. Source: AES Nation.

None of the private client lawyers in the survey met our income criteria for elite status, which is a consistent annual income of $1 million or more over five years. Therefore, we identified an additional cohort of 41 private client lawyers who have regularly earned $1 million or more each year over the previous half decade.

It's important to note that all the private client lawyers surveyed, including the 41 $1 million+ earners, are equity partners in their firms. However, the income numbers we are using are based solely on their individual legal practices. Compensation from their partnership interests or outside business interests is not included.

Looking across the three income segments of private client lawyers and supported by the extensive research we have conducted with other types of professionals focused on the wealthy, including wealth managers, multifamily offices and accountants, we were able to establish and verify many best practices, which we will share with you in Part III of this book.

As we present the survey data, you will frequently see that the perspectives and actions of the $1 million+ earners are notably different from those earning less than $600,000. Regardless of your own income level, these elite private client lawyers offer lessons for excelling in today's environment.

The matter of technical proficiency

To excel, you must be technically proficient. This is not just good business—it's a moral obligation. Nearly all the private client lawyers surveyed identify their technical proficiency to be critical to the success of their practices (see Exhibit 1.3).

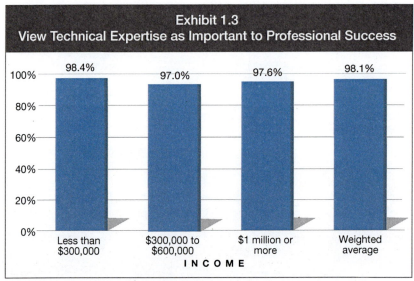

Exhibit 1.3
View Technical Expertise as Important to Professional Success

N = 359 private client lawyers. Source: AES Nation.

Without question, technical proficiency is extremely important—it is fundamental to the responsible practice of law. The primary objective of private client lawyers is, of course, to do the best job possible for their wealthy clients. But is a tremendous emphasis on technical proficiency the best way to build an exceptional high-net-worth legal practice?

Private client lawyers engaged by the wealthy are acknowledged as being technically adept or they would not be engaged. Despite the emphasis that many private client lawyers place on the importance and promotion of their technical competencies, it's often not in and of itself a determining selling point. Why? Because wealthy clients in general are unable to differentiate among private client lawyers based on their technical expertise.

The wealthy tend to hire private client lawyers to handle the legal nuances and complexities that are, for the most part, beyond them. This is why they rely heavily on other professionals they are working with when they need to find and select a private client lawyer—a topic we'll address in Chapter 7.

While technical proficiency is indeed critical to delivering the most appropriate high-quality legal strategies, you should avoid overemphasizing it or getting wrapped up in trying to prove your legal brilliance. Because technical proficiency is a given, it's usually not the best way to effectively differentiate yourself from competitors.

The importance of relationship management

So even if you are a genius-level technician, that is rarely enough to create an exceptional high-net-worth legal practice. You also need to be able to build high levels of personal rapport with your wealthy clients and to effectively communicate your true value to them.

In his book *Bleak House,* Charles Dickens describes Mr. Tulkinghorn, a private client lawyer, in this way: "He is surrounded by a mysterious halo of family confidences, of which he is known to be the silent depository." This description helps identify some of the nontechnical aspects of accomplished private client lawyers.

About four out of five of the private client lawyers surveyed expressed the importance of relationship management expertise (see Exhibit 1.4). The more financially successful private client lawyers recognized this in a slightly higher proportion.

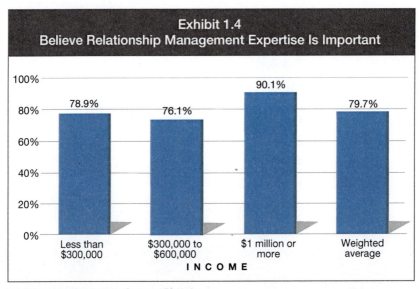

N = 359 private client lawyers. Source: AES Nation.

Relationship management encompasses several components. As Mr. Tulkinghorn demonstrated, discretion is essential, as high-net-worth clients must believe their secrets—including the sometimes-embarrassing intimate details of their lives—are safe with their lawyer.

Loyalty is also quite important, as these relationships can extend a long time—in some cases, for generations. The wealthy also want their private client lawyers to display appropriate humility and diplomatic skills.

There is no question that the wealthy want their private client lawyers to be technically competent. Given their druthers, they would prefer to engage legal savants—absolute masters of sophisticated and complex technical legal knowledge.

However, this is rarely enough. The wealthy also want to engage private client lawyers whom they want to know everything about them, including the less-than-pleasant family secrets. The wealthy must be comfortable discussing the intimacies of their lives, such as their drug-addicted children, their extramarital affairs or their self-destructive tendencies.

It is certainly a skill and a talent to create interpersonal trust with the wealthy. They tend to be wary of professionals, with good reason. Their suspiciousness is habitually born of experience. Because high-caliber private client lawyers often become involved in the "backstage" and even closeted activities of their high-net-worth clients, including being dragged into intrafamily conflicts, it is essential to engender confidence and promote interpersonal trust.

The takeaways

Private client lawyers play an important role in the lives of their high-net-worth clients. They directly deliver a collection of legal services in high demand by the wealthy. As such, they have an integral set of responsibilities and functions in the ecosystem of the wealthy. Although the best private client lawyers marry considerable technical expertise with extraordinary interpersonal skills, this is not characteristic across the profession.

As we will see in the following chapters, income variations are a very good way to segment private client lawyers, enabling us to ascertain best practices. In the next chapter, we will compare the perspectives and perceptions of private client lawyers about their profession.

CHAPTER 2

Living in Turbulent Times

When it comes to professional advisors who work with the wealthy, it's clear that all of them are in a state of flux. Recent research with wealth managers, senior executives in multifamily offices, high-end accountants and private bankers finds that each type of professional is having more concerns about achieving success. Their professions are facing headwinds, and consequently their livelihoods are in a state of unrest.

This is definitely the case in the world of private client lawyers. Overall, nine out of ten private client lawyers said that the legal business environment catering to the wealthy is turbulent (see Exhibit 2.1).

There are two viable approaches to dealing with the substantial and potentially negative changes in the world of private client lawyers. One is to hope and just keep doing what you are doing. You can hope that your legal practice will last long enough so that the sea changes in your profession will have minimal personal impact. This may mean that you are near the end of your career and are running down the clock, which can certainly be a smart and worthwhile approach to the matter.

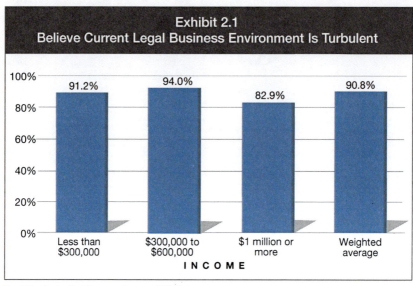

N = 359 private client lawyers. Source: AES Nation.

The other response is to proactively and cleverly adapt to the sea changes and make them work for you. By staying abreast of the changes in the private client legal business model, and then recognizing and capitalizing on opportunities as they present themselves, you can not only survive turbulent times but also significantly prosper—and set the stage to build serious wealth.

Key concerns

A number of issues are causing consternation among private client lawyers. We identified and evaluated six:

- Significantly increasing competition

- The commoditization of private client legal services

- Major adverse changes in tax law and planning strategies

- The cost sensitivity of high-net-worth clients

- Ability to access wealthy clients

- Downward pressure on incomes

Significantly increasing competition

More than four out of five surveyed private client lawyers reported that competition is significantly increasing (see Exhibit 2.2). This is somewhat less so among the elite private client lawyers.

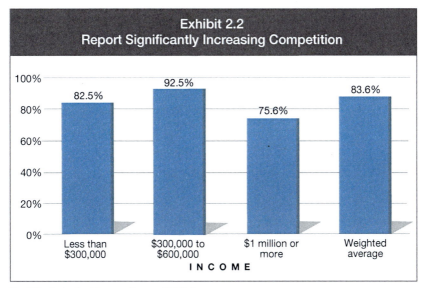

N = 359 private client lawyers. Source: AES Nation.

Competition—from peers, technology (especially in the form of artificial intelligence), and a plethora of non-legal professionals all ready and eager to provide various planning services—is definitely on the rise, with no letup in sight. Private client lawyers have a legal monopoly, but it does not extend beyond being a scribe, making all variations of planning services and other functions such as trusteeships open game.

Nevertheless, your ability as a private client lawyer to source the wealthy and be recognized for your know-how, coupled with the ability to deliver and communicate outstanding value, enables you to stand above the morass of prospective providers of planning and related services.

The commoditization of private client legal services

Law is a mature industry, which makes every private client lawyer replaceable. This does not mean some are not superior to others, for that certainly is the case. However, as all legitimate legal planning strategies can, in principal, be delivered by any high-quality private client lawyer, there are no proprietary alternatives. The result is that private client legal services—save possibly for intense, in-depth, one-off highly customized tax planning—are a commodity.

Nearly four out of five of those surveyed recognize this and view it as seriously unfavorable (see Exhibit 2.3). At the same time, we have discerned that the elite private client lawyers, although recognizing the growing commoditization of private client legal expertise, also recognize the ability to reach out, connect and build rapport with the wealthy to become the legal services provider of choice. In effect, many elite private client lawyers are overriding the problem of commoditization.

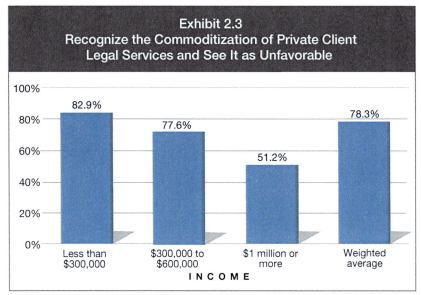

N = 359 private client lawyers. Source: AES Nation.

Major adverse changes in tax law and planning strategies

Another complicating factor in the world of legal services for the wealthy is when tax laws change and powerful planning strategies are negated. For example, what would happen to private client lawyers if major taxes were eliminated? As taxes are regularly cornerstones of the demand for private client legal services, their eradication could have a major adverse impact on the need for those services.

It turns out that the possibility or inevitability of major adverse changes in tax law or planning strategies is a big concern for about two-thirds of those surveyed (see Exhibit 2.4). It's less of a concern proportionately for private client lawyers earning $300,000 or less, as they are less likely to be working with wealthier clients. However, this is a bigger concern for those earning more and who are more dependent on wealthy clients motivated to minimize their taxes.

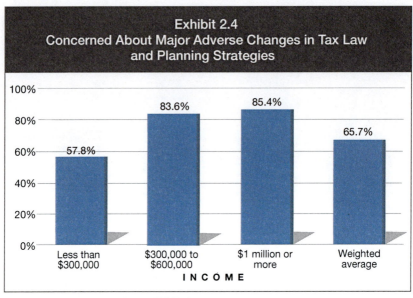

N = 359 private client lawyers. Source: AES Nation.

The cost sensitivity of high-net-worth clients

Another concern of private client lawyers is that their wealthy clients are increasingly sophisticated and demanding. As the wealthy—and this is more pronounced among the Super Rich and single-family offices—move up the learning curve and become more knowledgeable and discerning about what is available to them, they become more demanding. This often translates into greater price sensitivity and makes them more and more interested in verifiable, cost-effective results.

Overall, about 70 percent of those surveyed are finding their wealthy clients more cost-sensitive (see **Exhibit 2.5**). This is proportionately more the case with private client lawyers who earn less than $600,000. Among the elite private client lawyers, being able to deliver outstanding value and—extremely important—communicate that value tends to minimize their wealthy clients' trepidation over fees.

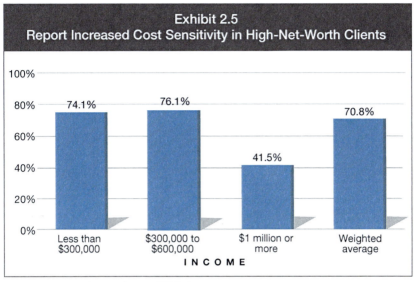

N = 359 private client lawyers. Source: AES Nation.

As we will see in Chapter 11, elite private client lawyers tend to use value-based project fees as opposed to the more traditional time + expenses fee structure. Aside from the fact that value-based project fees are strongly preferred by the wealthy, these fees also have the possibility of generating greater revenue than time + expenses fees.

Ability to access wealthy clients

Being able to connect with high-net-worth clients is a major concern for more than four out of five private client lawyers surveyed (see Exhibit 2.6). With increasingly commoditized expertise and intensifying competition, the ability to source high-value wealthy clients is a major cause of distress for many of them. Proportionately fewer of the elite private client lawyers are practically or emotionally encumbered by any perceived inability to source the wealthy.

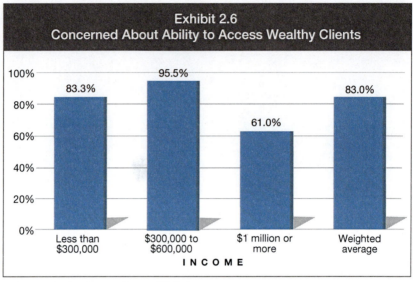

N = 359 private client lawyers. Source: AES Nation.

There are empirically and field-proven methodologies for accessing the wealthy, such as street-smart networking (which we will discuss in Chapter 7). These processes work across the entire high-net-worth landscape. If you can effectively employ these methodologies, they often can bring in a steady stream of new high-net-worth clients and consequently help you build an exceptional high-net-worth legal practice that leads to serious wealth.

Downward pressure on incomes

Three-quarters of private client lawyers report that the current turbulent environment is putting downward pressure on their incomes (see **Exhibit 2.7**). This is somewhat more pronounced for those earning $300,000 to $600,000 annually. In effect, they feel that it is very difficult or that they cannot squeeze any more money out of their legal practices. This concern was identified by only a quarter of the private client lawyers earning $1 million or more annually.

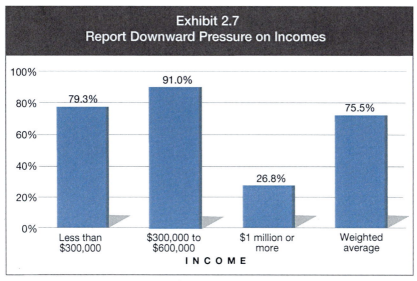

N = 359 private client lawyers. Source: AES Nation.

Downward pressure on incomes is highly correlated with diminished lifestyles. The result for many is that the practice of law on behalf of high-net-worth clients is a wasting asset. But this need not be the case!

Dark clouds ahead

Overall, most private client lawyers see the current business environment as challenging. A number of factors are working against them, resulting in lower incomes and the possibility of a reduced lifestyle. We also found that the private client lawyers surveyed believe it is only going to get harder to excel (see Exhibit 2.8).

It will be a matter of working hard, but also working very smart. Because of the incredible boom in the creation of personal fortunes, private client lawyers who are willing to put in the requisite hours running their legal practices efficiently while adopting best practices are quite likely to excel even as the business environment for their legal expertise becomes more difficult.

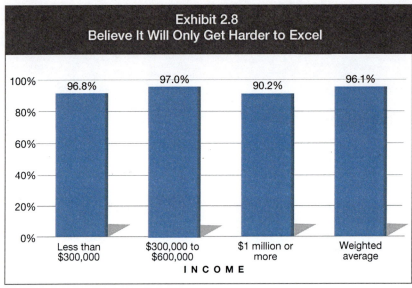

N = 359 private client lawyers. Source: AES Nation.

While nearly all the private client lawyers see the dark clouds, if you can see and act on the ways to connect with and deliver value to the wealthy, you will probably prosper disproportionately. You will be among the ones who will collect the gold at the end of the rainbow.

The takeaways

In challenging times, there are always opportunities. Many of your peers may rage and retreat, but the more forward-thinking and business-savvy ones will determine ways to better serve the wealthy, and they will profit by doing so. We want you to be in the second group.

EXCELLING IN TURBULENT TIMES

There is no question that the world of the private client lawyer is in transition. It's a turbulent time to be a legal professional in the service of the wealthy. For many of them, it feels like it's harder to be as successful as they were in the past or even to become successful. Many private client lawyers are running faster just to stay in place, and the future does not look a whole lot brighter. Making this personal, a meaningful number of private client lawyers fear that their incomes are likely to profoundly decrease, putting downward pressure on their lifestyles.

The unease they feel is justified. All of their concerns are very real, and each interacts, amplifying the others. The outlook for many private client lawyers is far from rosy; in fact, it can be quite grim. But all is far from hopeless. This near-apocalyptic viewpoint is not characteristic of all private client lawyers and certainly need not be their professional future.

By artfully adopting the best practices of the elite private client lawyers in conjunction with the lessons learned from other elite professionals, you could potentially create an exceptional high-net-worth legal practice that can conceivably make you seriously wealthy.

We have talked about private client lawyers building significant wealth. But just what does that mean? In the next chapter, we will explain what it takes to become seriously wealthy.

CHAPTER 3

Building Significant Wealth

If you are like many private client lawyers, you have an ingrained drive to excel. Building serious wealth is an important goal for many—if not most—capable, skilled and determined professionals.

There are many intertwined reasons for this. Sometimes it's a matter of ego or simply greed, but—in our experience and backed by previous research across a wide array of accomplished individuals—the motivations are usually much more noble. Still, for whatever reasons, many private client lawyers want to be wealthier.

The desire to become seriously wealthy

Of the private client lawyers surveyed, the higher their annual incomes, the more they want to be meaningfully wealthier (see Exhibit 3.1). Overall, almost 80 percent want to be seriously wealthy. This goal is shared by all the highest-earning private client lawyers.

Defining serious wealth can be complicated. For almost everyone, it is being worth more—often a lot more—than you are worth today. The person with a net worth of $1 million will regularly say being seriously wealthy requires a net worth of $10 million or more. Likewise, a person with a net worth of $10 million will say serious wealth means a net worth of $50 million or more.

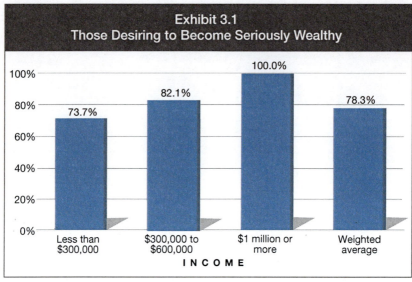

Exhibit 3.1
Those Desiring to Become Seriously Wealthy

N = 359 private client lawyers. Source: AES Nation.

Based on extensive assessments of the wealthy—very broadly speaking—a person is seriously wealthy if he or she has a net worth of $20 million or more. A net worth of $20 million is sometimes called "jet plane money," as it eliminates the need to fly commercial.

The desire to become seriously wealthy is very common. In an extensive survey of 262 successful business owners (those with financial assets of $1 million or more on top of the equity in their business and other assets such as a house), almost 95 percent of them want to be wealthier (see Exhibit 3.2).

People often want to become seriously wealthy for reasons beyond themselves. This was very evident in our research of the 247 successful business owners who want to be wealthier (see Exhibit 3.3).

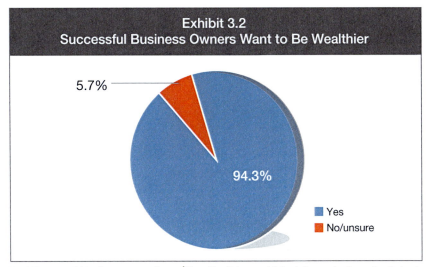

N = 262 successful business owners. Source: Russ Alan Prince and John J. Bowen Jr., *Becoming Seriously Wealthy: How to Harness the Strategies of the Super Rich and Ultra-Wealthy Business Owners*, 2017.

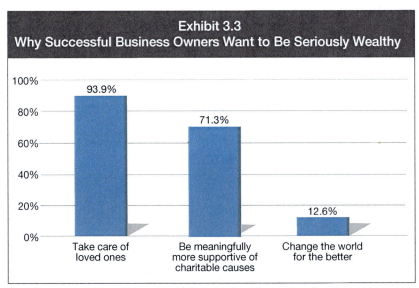

N = 247 successful business owners who want to be wealthier. Source: Russ Alan Prince and John J. Bowen Jr., *Becoming Seriously Wealthy: How to Harness the Strategies of the Super Rich and Ultra-Wealthy Business Owners*, 2017.

Greater wealth will not eliminate problems, but it can be very helpful in solving many of them. Most people accept their responsibilities and seek to help those they care about. Moving beyond their own intimate worlds, many people want to be philanthropic. Supporting causes that are dear to them is a viable way to better society, the planet and the lives of others. Some people supercharge this concept and strive to change the world for the better.

As we can see in Exhibit 3.3, the great majority of successful business owners strive for greater personal fortunes with the aims of making a more meaningful difference in the lives of people close to them and to be more supportive of their charitable causes. A smaller percentage are aiming even higher and thinking globally. This is a far cry from desiring significant wealth because of ego or greed.

When we have empirically delved into this issue, we have consistently found that most business owners, professionals and even the Super Rich are motivated to become wealthier for reasons of caring and concern. In all probability, this is the same with the great majority of private client lawyers including, most likely, you.

What will it take to become seriously wealthy?

There are many ways to amass a significant personal fortune. For example, Pablo Escobar earned a place on the Forbes list of billionaires for seven years in a row from 1987 to 1993. In 1989, he was the seventh-richest person in the world with an estimated net worth of $30 billion. His organization generated approximately $420 million per week, or almost $22 billion each year. Being the head of a phenomenally brutal drug cartel can make someone astoundingly wealthy. There are usually complications, however. In Pablo Escobar's case, the Columbian National Police killed him a day after his 44th birthday.

There are many other illegal ways to strike it rich—even very, very rich. But let's be very clear: Anything that is in any way illicit should absolutely be avoided. Stay far away from any illegal activities and morally questionable activities as well. For instance, private client lawyers using their expertise to facilitate protecting the assets of unscrupulous and ruthless individuals may not be illegal, depending on jurisdictions, but should be avoided just the same.

Another way—which is not at all illegal—to potentially become seriously wealthy is to marry money. While the media periodically shows examples of this, it is unlikely to be a very effective personal wealth generation strategy for most people, including most private client lawyers. Still another way to become seriously wealthy is winning the lottery where the prize after taxes is $20 million or more. Inheriting a sizable fortune is akin to winning the lottery.

However, to get on the track to serious wealth, you, along with the great majority of private client lawyers, probably need to start with your legal practice. As it is for the successful and ultra-wealthy business owners and most of the Super Rich, the foundation of personal wealth for most private client lawyers is their profession.

Our empirical research and extensive experience in working with private client lawyers have shown us what is most effective in building exceptional high-net-worth legal practices. We will delve into best practices extensively in Part III of this book, but for now, keep these goals at the forefront:

- **Source wealthy clients.** Being able to access the wealthy is essential to build an exceptional high-net-worth legal practice. The highest-potential wealthy clients for most private client lawyers are successful business owners.

- **Become a recognized legal authority for a segment of the wealthy.** Being a thought leader is a powerful way to effectively differentiate yourself. It's like being brilliantly backlit.

- **Develop a deep understanding of your wealthy clients.** The better you understand the dreams, anxieties, expectations and limitations of your wealthy clients, the more effective you usually are. Unfortunately, most private client lawyers tend to profile their wealthy clientele somewhat myopically.

- **Maximize the legal and financial relationships with wealthy clients.** It is typically not easy to source a wealthy client, so it makes good business sense to deliver as much value as possible. This will often require moving beyond your own legal expertise by bringing in other types of lawyers and advisors.

- **Communicate the outstanding value provided to wealthy clients.** This entails not only delivering exceptional legal expertise, but also ensuring that your wealthy clients understand the value they are receiving. Legal brilliance does not exist in this environment unless the wealthy and their other advisors say it does.

- **Be appropriately compensated.** The traditional fee structure based on time + expenses is, in many ways, anathema to the wealthy. A viable solution is value-based project fees and in some cases retainer fees. Moreover, by employing these alternatives, you may well be able to obtain premium pricing.

By running a high-net-worth legal practice in this way, you will probably be able to create a substantial financial base. Will this result in serious wealth? Maybe. Will it lead to a meaningful increase in your annual revenue? Almost always!

As we will see in later chapters, most private client lawyers are not doing nearly as good a job as they could when it comes to these matters. By adopting the best practices of elite private client lawyers (those earning $1 million or more annually) and other elite professionals catering to the wealthy, you may very well be able to upgrade or refine your high-net-worth legal practice, resulting in far greater revenue.

While our focus in this book is on helping private client lawyers become more professionally successful, another factor in building significant wealth is often critical. You would be well-advised to maximize your *personal* wealth.

For example, in working with successful business owners to build serious wealth, we have found that relatively few of them are using the myriad tax and legal strategies and the financial products that can result in much greater personal fortunes. We call these wealth management products and services Super Rich Solutions. These findings, as well as examples of some Super Rich Solutions, are detailed in our book *Becoming Seriously Wealthy: How to Harness the Strategies of the Super Rich and Ultra-Wealthy Business Owners* (2017).

As with many successful business owners, we consistently find a substantial proportion of private client lawyers are not acting to maximize their personal wealth. So to become seriously wealthy, aside from making your high-net-worth legal practice markedly more successful, you should evaluate your personal financial situation and, if appropriate, take steps to protect and grow your wealth while mitigating taxes.

Some of this would entail making use of your legal expertise. However, as the phrase goes, "The cobbler's children have no shoes." While many private client lawyers provide creative and impressive legal strategies to their wealthy clients, resulting in greater personal wealth and structures to protect that wealth, many of them fail to implement such strategies for themselves.

A substantial percentage of private client lawyers would also likely benefit from the services of a high-caliber wealth manager. Product-based solutions, such as sophisticated qualified retirement plans, captive insurance companies and private placement life insurance can all conceivably prove highly advantageous to those seeking to amass sizable personal fortunes.

The takeaways

It's fair to say that many private client lawyers want to become seriously wealthy, or at least significantly wealthier than they are today. There are many reasons for this and, very likely, most of those reasons revolve around:

- Caring for loved ones

- Supporting charitable causes

- Changing the world for the better

Whatever your own motivation to become wealthier, your ability to do so probably starts with making your high-net-worth legal practice as successful as possible. This involves accessing the wealthy and delivering recognizable and appreciated high-quality legal strategies. It may also involve employing tax and other types of planning coupled with wealth management products that enable you to maximize your personal wealth.

All other things being equal, the more affluent and need-driven your clientele, the better for your practice. For many private client lawyers, this means focusing on the engines of private wealth creation: successful business owners and their companies. We will address these in the next chapter.

PART II

In the Line of Money: Today's High-Net-Worth Client Opportunities

To become seriously wealthy, you must concentrate your efforts on high-net-worth clients who can benefit from your legal knowledge and skills including, but not restricted to, private client legal services. These clients must also be able and willing to pay for your expertise. Focusing on these types of high-net-worth clients is called being "in the line of money."

As we will see, the optimal client for the great majority of private client lawyers is the successful business owner. These accomplished entrepreneurs can be exceedingly lucrative for private client lawyers, as well as for the other types of lawyers who can be brought in to address company and other types of personal matters.

Meanwhile, single-family offices are potentially the most profitable type of high-net-worth client. However, compared to successful business owners, they are often harder to work with, as they frequently require diverse legal expertise and are much, much more difficult to source.

EXCELLING IN TURBULENT TIMES

There are many other types of wealthy clients, from C-level corporate executives to affluent art collectors, moneyed inheritors and renowned celebrities. The key is that to have a chance at building serious wealth for yourself, you must make sure you are firmly *in the line of money.*

CHAPTER 4

The Engine of Private Wealth Creation: Successful Business Owners

To have an exceptional high-net-worth legal practice, you need wealthy clients who require your expertise and can afford your services. And the more other types of legal services that you can indirectly deliver, the more successful you will be.

For example, being able to offer—by bringing in other lawyers—matrimonial and family services, exit planning expertise and even litigation capabilities can all contribute greatly to the monetary success of a high-net-worth legal practice.

Other factors come into play. For instance, you can add more value when a high-net-worth client's circumstances are more complex and correlate with high levels of personal wealth. Complicated situations tend to require more effort and more varied legal expertise. Based on these criteria, successful business owners and their companies are often the preferred—if not optimal—type of wealthy client.

Preferred clients of private client lawyers

Based on previous empirical investigations and backed up by our coaching and consulting experience with elite private client lawyers, we know that their financial success is very frequently a function of working with successful business owners. Our perspective is validated by nearly 60 percent of those surveyed (see Exhibit 4.1).

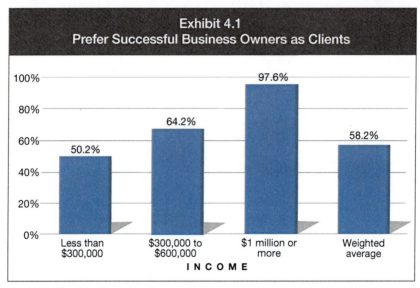

Exhibit 4.1
Prefer Successful Business Owners as Clients

N = 359 private client lawyers. Source: AES Nation.

For these private client lawyers, there is no question that their preferred clients are business owners, which also potentially includes the clients' companies. And the more private client lawyers earn, the more likely they are to see successful business owners as preferred clients.

In considering all high-net-worth families, successful business owners are an exceedingly profitable segment. But they are a diverse bunch. Consider these three groups:

- Owners of family businesses

- Owners of privately held companies

- Owners of professional practices

These categories of business owners can be further divided. Family-owned businesses, for example, could be segmented by the different generations. Owners of professional practices could be categorized by the nature of their professions, such as health care, legal and consulting.

Because business owners have an equity stake in successful commercial enterprises, they are pursuing the most assured way of building considerable personal wealth. For the most part, successful business owners are the optimal clients for the great majority of private client lawyers.

To better understand the considerable business potential, let's look at some of the services they need and want.

Extensive multiple opportunities provided by successful business owners

Accomplished business owners and their companies are the ideal pool of high-net-worth clients for most private client lawyers because these entrepreneurs and their closely held companies are the undisputed drivers of great personal wealth. Also, successful business owner clients commonly have complicated and involved situations, often requiring extensive and diverse legal services.

Returning to the research we conducted with 262 successful business owners, we found that many of them are probably in considerable need of high-caliber private client legal services. For example, nearly nine out of ten successful business owners have an estate plan, which is defined as having, at a minimum, a will (see Exhibit 4.2).

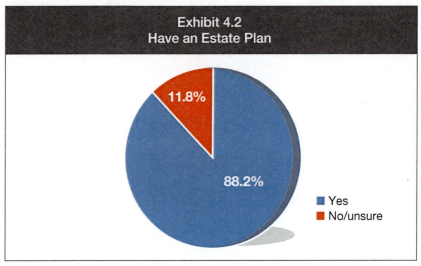

N = 262 successful business owners. Source: Russ Alan Prince and John J. Bowen Jr., *Becoming Seriously Wealthy: How to Harness the Strategies of the Super Rich and Ultra-Wealthy Business Owners*, 2017.

However, of those successful business owners who do have estate plans, about 85 percent of them are more than five years old (see Exhibit 4.3). Because of continual changes in the tax laws and in the lives of the business owners, estate plans more than a few years old likely fail to take maximum advantage of available opportunities and/or are not designed to meet the current needs of the high-net-worth family.

Along the same lines, more than 85 percent of successful business owners are concerned about being involved in unjust lawsuits or being victimized in malicious divorce proceedings (see Exhibit 4.4). However, just a little more than a quarter of them have formal asset protection plans (see Exhibit 4.5).

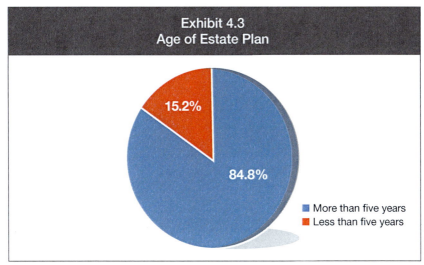

N = 231 successful business owners. Source: Russ Alan Prince and John J. Bowen Jr., *Becoming Seriously Wealthy: How to Harness the Strategies of the Super Rich and Ultra-Wealthy Business Owners*, 2017.

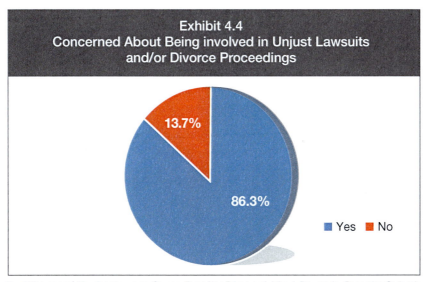

N = 262 successful business owners. Source: Russ Alan Prince and John J. Bowen Jr., *Becoming Seriously Wealthy: How to Harness the Strategies of the Super Rich and Ultra-Wealthy Business Owners*, 2017.

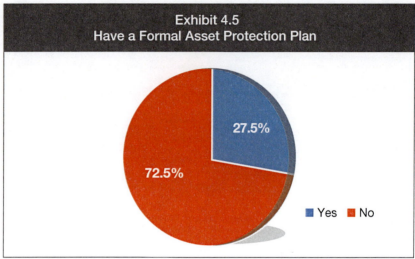

N = 262 successful business owners. Source: Russ Alan Prince and John J. Bowen Jr., *Becoming Seriously Wealthy: How to Harness the Strategies of the Super Rich and Ultra-Wealthy Business Owners*, 2017.

Clearly, a great many successful business owners can benefit both personally and financially from the knowledge and skills of a high-caliber private client lawyer. At the same time, they regularly offer tremendous opportunities because of the companies they own and often run.

These business owners require and commonly request a range of additional legal services. Some of these services lie outside the private client legal realm, such as:

- Facilitating corporate wealth management solutions

- Corporate exit planning

- Mergers and acquisitions

- Marital and family

- Intellectual property

- Commercial litigation

- Human resources

- Real estate

Working with successful business owners has additional advantages. For example, they tend to be decision-makers. Not only do they have authority, but also—for better or worse—they usually make decisions rapidly, as opposed to contemplating and considering and then re-contemplating and reconsidering possibilities. The result is that they often make choices comparatively quickly.

The takeaways

If you are intent on building your wealth, seriously consider concentrating much of your efforts on accessing and delivering a range of appropriate high-quality legal services to successful business owners and the firms they control. The revenue and lifetime client value possibilities from this type of high-net-worth client tend to dwarf the possibilities from most other types of high-net-worth clients.

To excel with successful business owners or any other type of high-net-worth client, you must be able to provide powerful legal services and do so in areas where the wealthy recognize and appreciate the value you deliver. Many factors make this all work, which we will discuss when we address best practices.

EXCELLING IN TURBULENT TIMES

Although successful business owners and their companies are very often optimal clients for private client lawyers aspiring to become seriously wealthy, they are not the only high-potential clients. In the next chapter, we will briefly look at the wealthiest people in the world and the firms they establish to help manage their fortunes and their lives.

CHAPTER 5

The Apex of the Pyramid: The Super Rich and Single-Family Offices

For most private client lawyers, successful business owners are assuredly the best type of high-net-worth client. Not only do their level of personal affluence and their often-complex situations provide substantial possibilities for personal legal services, but their companies often need an array of diverse legal expertise.

Still, for a select few private client lawyers, their focus is on the apex of the financial pyramid—the richest of the rich. They want to garner the Super Rich and the boutique firms—the single-family offices—that address the extremely wealthy's financial and lifestyle needs and wants.

For capable private client lawyers, these astoundingly wealthy clients can be the most profitable of all. The wealth they control is amazing, and their lives are often quite multifarious. This mix of attributes commonly requires wide-ranging—and many times intricate and sophisticated—legal services.

Elite private client lawyers focus on the Super Rich and single-family offices

Even though the Super Rich and single-family offices can be amazingly profitable for private client lawyers, only 3.4 percent of those surveyed are actively looking and taking steps to cultivate them (see Exhibit 5.1).

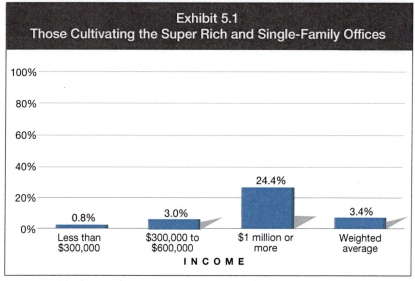

Exhibit 5.1
Those Cultivating the Super Rich and Single-Family Offices

N = 359 private client lawyers. Source: AES Nation.

Just two private client lawyers earning less than $300,000 annually and two earning between $300,000 and $600,000 annually are concentrating some of their energies and resources on cultivating the Super Rich and single-family offices. Meanwhile, a quarter of those earning $1 million or more are working to access these types of wealthy clients and are making concerted efforts to win them over.

Single-family offices tend to have a special appeal to a broad array of advisors as they usually have professional management that can result in more astute and faster decision-making. The single-family office itself can be understood as a family business that consistently requires a multitude of legal services. Furthermore, a substantial percentage of exceptionally wealthy families with single-family offices have ongoing business interests aside from the single-family office. This creates further opportunities for private client lawyers to deliver their legal expertise and the legal services of other types of lawyers.

In extensive research and consulting with single-family offices, we find a greater and greater tendency to outsource various kinds of expertise. This bodes very well for private client lawyers.

Single-family offices outsourcing legal expertise

The costs of running a single-family office have always been an issue, but the exceptionally wealthy have been scrutinizing those costs even more closely since 2008. Both exceptionally wealthy families with existing single-family offices and the Super Rich new to single-family offices have deduced that doing everything internally can all too easily become a massively expensive headache. Moreover, for a great many single-family offices, doing everything in-house never seems to produce optimal or even desired results.

The aim of getting optimal results has led to the rise of strategic outsourcing. Figuring out which forms of expertise to keep internal and which to farm out is a critical role of senior management at these single-family offices. When a private client lawyer can provide at a reasonable price legal expertise at a higher level of quality and excellence than can be provided in-house, and provide it without conflict and with transparency, senior executives at single-family offices have been strongly inclined to engage those private client lawyers on an outsourced basis to best serve the exceptionally wealthy family's needs and objectives.

With strategic outsourcing becoming more and more common, most senior executives of single-family offices are inclined to turn to external talented and recognized legal authorities. The way these senior executives make provider decisions highlights the importance of being a thought leader (a topic we will discuss in Chapter 8).

The spectrum of legal services

Single-family offices obtain a great number of legal services from lawyers. Aside from all the expertise provided by private client lawyers, there are numerous other opportunities to deliver legal services, such as:

- **Matrimonial.** Members of exceptionally wealthy families tend to have considerable need for matrimonial legal services, from preparing prenuptial agreements to negotiating divorces and arranging settlements.

- **Corporate finance.** With the growing appeal of direct investments, "club deals" and co-investments with pension funds, and even sovereign wealth funds, single-family offices rely on expert legal corporate finance advice.

- **Tax controversy.** All manner of disagreements over taxes with governments potentially need to be addressed by tax law specialists.

- Real estate. **Lawyers are required to address the real estate** acquisitions and investments of the exceptionally wealthy. These range from their homes to the land connected with operating business to investments in real estate.

- **Litigation.** Both commercial and personal litigation—which is not uncommon among the exceptionally wealthy—require the services of top-flight trial lawyers.

- **Government relations.** From supporting business interests to addressing changing laws and regulations, a percentage of single-family offices engage lawyers to provide access to and assist in dealing with government functionaries.

To work successfully with single-family offices and the exceptionally wealthy families they serve, private client lawyers must have very strong relationships with their clients and access to tremendous legal talent in these different areas. When this is the case, each single-family office can easily represent many millions of dollars in revenue to private client lawyers and the legal talent they bring in.

Evolving versions of single-family offices

There are also ample opportunities to provide legal services directly to the single-family offices that are created by their need to constantly update and evolve—for they, too, are operating in turbulent times.

When managed well, single-family offices are structurally flexible. This permits them to readily adapt to changing circumstances. There is a tremendous amount of variation between the all-in self-contained single-family office—which is rare—and the completely virtual single-family office. Consider these examples:

- **Hub-and-spoke.** The inheritors set up a "satellite" single-family office focused on managing their investments while the parents' single-family office provides the administrative support, legal expertise and lifestyle services. This results in the inheritors maintaining many of the advantages of a full-service single-family office without having to duplicate a variety of desired deliverables.

- **Private investment companies.** The private investment company is gaining attention as successful hedge fund managers choose to disgorge investor monies in favor of just running their own wealth. When hedge funds become single-family offices, except in a few cases, they are often converting to a private investment company, as money management is their only intent. The reason they are referred to as family offices is a legal one. After establishing their private investment companies, a percentage of these firms choose to incorporate more deliverables into their operations, making them multi-service single-family offices.

- **Near-virtual single-family office.** Technology has made the near-virtual single-family office possible. This can be attractive because of the low cost structure as most of the expenses are variable. Near-virtual single-family offices can vary in complexity. For example, on the more complex end of the spectrum, we designed and helped implement a near-virtual single-family office for a perpetual tourist.

The single-family office model will continue to adapt in response to the evolving requirements of the Super Rich. These adjustments require the expertise of private client lawyers.

Counting the Super Rich and single-family offices

As we talk about the tremendous potential of single-family office clients, a key question frequently arises: "How many Super Rich families and single-family offices are there?" It's a valid and interesting question, which unfortunately lacks a definitive answer.

A number of consulting organizations calculate the size of the private wealth market. Consulting firms such as the Boston Consulting Group and Capgemini regularly produce reports on the industry, including their estimates of the number of wealthy individuals. Wealth-X is another firm that produces such information.

When it comes to calculating the size of the private wealth universe, these consulting firms and others employ a range of well-reasoned methodologies to produce their numbers. The conundrums are not with the methodologies but the assumptions that underpin the methodologies and the resources they can deploy to ferret out the Super Rich. The results are usually very scholarly estimates and well-researched lists. But they are certainly estimates, and the various lists can differ substantially.

Consider the number of billionaires. Depending on whose calculations are used, estimates of the number of billionaires in the world today range between 1,700 and 2,100. What is very telling is that none of these estimates likely included Sergei Roldugin. Who is Sergei Roldugin?

In 2014, Sergei Roldugin informed the *New York Times* that he did not have millions of dollars. Then the Panama Papers came along, and Sergei (or at least his name) was connected to $2 billion located in an interlaced network of offshore companies. The Panama Papers named some individuals who are not being counted by the firms tracking the Super Rich.

As for single-family offices, industry pundits provide estimates ranging from 2,000 to 15,000 throughout the world. Without question, a plethora of single-family offices intentionally hide from view. We are very confident there are more than 2,000 single-family offices, as we have a database of slightly more than 2,000 verified single-family offices and are certain our database does not contain all of them. Moreover, using a liberal definition of a single-family office, there will probably end up being more than 15,000 of them.

In all likelihood, the number of wealthy people is greater in number—especially when it comes to the Super Rich and single-family offices—than is calculated by the consulting firms. Single-family offices, the Super Rich and even those much less affluent have been known to hire private client lawyers and other professionals to muddle and even hide their affluence, making the process of counting them increasingly difficult. Nevertheless, the strong consensus is that the numbers of single-family offices and the Super Rich are growing, along with the amount of wealth they control.

Even though there is a populist critique of and, in some ways, a revolt against the Super Rich, there is absolutely no question that for the foreseeable future, the number of families joining the ranks of the Super Rich as well as the number of single-family offices is only going to multiply. Additionally, the sizes of their fortunes are likely to be greater than ever.

When it comes to creating an exceptional high-net-worth legal practice, a handful of these families or firms as clients can produce incredible revenues. Moreover, a private client lawyer—depending on the services provided and the closeness of the relationship—can effectively work with only a handful of Super Rich families and single-family offices at a time.

To succeed with these extremely high-net-worth clients, you must often be able to deliver sophisticated legal expertise. Moreover, to deliver this sophisticated legal expertise, you must gain access to these clients. To this end, it is critical to master some of the best practices we will discuss in the next section.

The takeaways

We can determine with great accuracy which of the various types of high-net-worth clients have tremendous potential for private client lawyers. While the Super Rich and single-family offices likely have the greatest potential, they are often the hardest to access and can be quite problematic to work with. They also require tremendous and usually diverse, sometimes esoteric, legal expertise. Another roadblock is that there are not—while precise numbers are unknown—that many of them worldwide.

In contrast to the Super Rich and single-family offices, a vast multitude of successful business owners are generally much, much easier to source and work with. They too are looking for the best legal strategies, and these strategies are often much more common. Successful business owners tend to make decisions relatively quickly, another reason why so many private client lawyers—especially those with greater incomes—are focused on this type of high-net-worth client.

Successful business owners, the Super Rich and single-family offices are not the only prospective clients for private client lawyers. In the next chapter, we will look at some other types of high-net-worth clients as well as some technical specialties that overlap various types of wealthy clients.

CHAPTER 6
More High-Net-Worth Client Opportunities

As we have seen, successful business owners are the most accessible and profitable type of high-net-worth client for a large percentage of private client lawyers. Not surprisingly, most private client lawyers consider successful business owners to be their preferred type of high-net-worth client.

For those private client lawyers with the extensive technical expertise, experience, industry profile and connections, the Super Rich and single-family offices are very much commercially worthwhile high-net-worth clients. But there are other types of high-net-worth clients that may be appealing to you.

More types of high-net-worth clients

While business owners and their companies are the engines of private wealth creation that typically require extensive private client legal services as well as other kinds of legal services, they are not the only viable types of clients for private client lawyers (see Exhibit 6.1).

Exhibit 6.1
Other Types of High-Net-Worth Clients Seen as Attractive

Type	INCOME			
	Less than $300,000	$300,000 to $600,000	$1 million or more	Weighted average
Corporate executives/ employees	67.7%	58.2%	4.9%	58.8%
Inheritors	9.6%	14.9%	7.3%	10.3%
Celebrities	4.4%	9.0%	2.4%	5.0%

N = 359 private client lawyers. Source: AES Nation.

Corporate executives and employees of companies are appealing to nearly 60 percent of those surveyed, though they are much more attractive to the private client lawyers earning less. For the highest-earning private client lawyers, the corporate executives they work with are usually all C-level with very complicated situations.

One out of ten of those surveyed sees inheritors as being a very attractive type of high-net-worth client. Private client lawyers earning between $300,000 and $600,000 are proportionately more interested in inheritors. Five percent of private client lawyers are focused on celebrity entertainers and athletes. This is very much a function of the quite limited number of celebrities who are really wealthy. Still, a lot of work can be done with celebrities, such as making very smart use of their loan-out corporations or similar vehicles to help maximize their wealth.

And there are still more possible types of high-net-worth clients.

Catering to wealthy fine art collectors

Many of the wealthy acquire fine art and other high-end collectibles, some because it is their passion and some as a hedge against economic uncertainty and financial volatility. For some of the wealthy, fine art, for example, helps define their personal identity. For others, being a fine art collector creates a sense of pride and satisfaction. For many wealthy fine art collectors, the investment potential of fine art is a powerful motivator. It's a way to add diversification to their investment portfolios and is often seen as a safe haven for wealth.

For those high-net-worth clients with substantial fine art collections, legal advice on an array of related matters can be a necessity. For example, estate planning must consider and address what are often thorny issues. For example, in transferring ownership of a fine art collection to the next generation, a slew of questions must be addressed, such as:

- Who will own it, and how will it be owned?

- Where are the monies to maintain and protect the collection?

- How are family conflicts over ownership and access avoided?

Private client lawyers are often not only involved with the mechanics of transferring art, but with setting and papering the parameters of use and control. For instance, in creating governance systems for family collections, private client lawyers deal with everything from structuring the legal entities to integrating the family agenda for the fine art collection into their family constitution. Private client lawyers can also play a role in the buying and selling of fine art. From 1031 exchanges to when the wealthy co-invest with art dealers, auction houses or other high-net-worth individuals, there is a major legal component.

For the exceptionally wealthy, moving upscale to a private museum is an option. Today, there are more than 300 privately funded fine art museums around the globe, most established since 2000. Some of the people who have established private museums include Eli and Edythe Broad, Carlos Slim, David Walsh, Kwee Swie Teng and Alice Walton. The role of private client lawyers in these arrangements is usually essential.

In our survey of private client lawyers, about 6 percent of them are catering to wealthy fine art collectors (see Exhibit 6.2). A significantly higher percentage of highest-earning private client lawyers are involved in this area. While this is a small niche, it can be a very lucrative one.

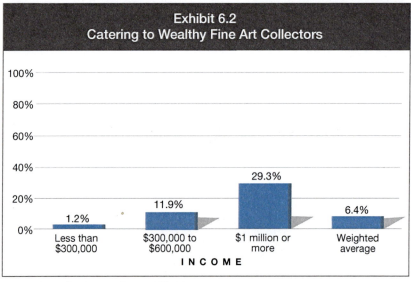

N = 359 private client lawyers. Source: AES Nation.

In the service of multi-territorial high-net-worth clients

Private client lawyers working with the globe-trotting wealthy are consistently able to generate disproportionately higher revenues. Many of the Super Rich and single-family offices require this expertise, as do a number of successful business owners, because they have assets and liabilities worldwide.

Private client lawyers in these situations must deal with hypermobile capital, meaning it is not locked down within any particular geography. In fact, the ability of these high-net-worth families to legitimately capitalize on the gaps in the laws and regulations of countries enables them to amass truly dazzling personal fortunes. This can happen in many ways, such as:

- Taking advantage of tax and regulatory arbitrage opportunities

- Creating custom cross-border business-to-business solutions

- Achieving more tax-efficient divorce settlements

- Acquiring luxury assets officially domiciled in offshore centers

- Obtaining multiple residences and passports

Another way private client lawyers prove essential to their multi-territorial clients is by helping them create a global wealth defense. This might include:

- "Stacking" trusts in multiple countries

- Using custom-made international structures and special purpose vehicles

- Benefiting from highly sophisticated and intricate legal strategies only available to this cohort, such as the "floating island" asset protection strategy

As working with multi-territorial clients requires distinctive technical knowledge and skills, it's not surprising that as few as one in ten of the private client lawyers surveyed works with these high-net-worth clients (see Exhibit 6.3). Moreover, a much higher percentage of the private client lawyers earning $1 million or more are dealing with these exceptionally wealthy global families.

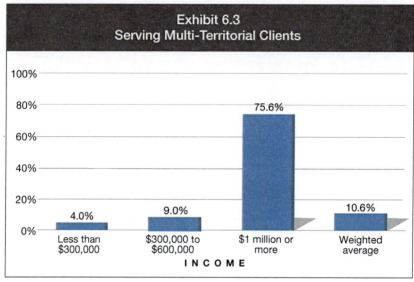

N = 359 private client lawyers. Source: AES Nation.

Private client lawyers are also profiting in this sphere by facilitating multinational capital flows. In effect, they are helping high-net-worth clients—especially extremely wealthy multi-territorial clients—come into compliance with the law.

With governments rightly cracking down on abuses, those high-net-worth individuals who took very liberal interpretations of some of the rules and regulations are motivated to readjust their positions and their wealth. Doing so requires the assistance of private client lawyers who are expert in this particular field. The application of this expertise ensuring alignment between the wealthy and governments is often a very powerful way to preserve significant family fortunes. Facilitating multinational capital flows is a booming business for skillful and knowledgeable private client lawyers.

Besides focusing on different types of high-net-worth clients, additional areas can be instrumental in building an exceptional high-net-worth legal practice and consequently building serious wealth. Two areas gaining a great deal of attention because of their revenue potential are enhancing the offerings of financial advisors—in effect, facilitating Super Rich Solutions—and addressing the adverse impact of great wealth on the family. It's important to keep in mind that all the different types of high-net-worth clients are prospective clients for both these areas of expertise.

Facilitating Super Rich Solutions

A large percentage of financial advisors are focusing on cultivating the wealthy. In our extensive research study of 803 financial advisors discussed in *Becoming Seriously Wealthy: How to Harness the Strategies of the Super Rich and Ultra-Wealthy Business Owners,* we found that relatively few are truly capable when it comes to delivering Super Rich Solutions. This creates a substantial opportunity for private client lawyers who want to scale their practices.

What are Super Rich Solutions?

We define Super Rich Solutions as wealth management strategies and products that many ultra-wealthy business owners, the Super Rich and single-family offices will use, when appropriate, to maximize personal wealth.

To be very clear, while we call them Super Rich Solutions because many of the wealthy can profit from them, this does not mean someone must be

Super Rich or even ultra-wealthy to significantly benefit from using them. For example, the various wealth management strategies and products we discussed in *Becoming Seriously Wealthy* can be used by many business owners to significantly increase or protect their personal wealth and, in some cases, improve the financial performance of their companies.

Astute private client lawyers who can support and enhance the delivery of Super Rich Solutions for wealthy clients have enormous business development opportunities. What clearly came out in the research was that the expertise of private client lawyers is needed in many situations because a substantial percentage of financial advisors are not very adept when it comes to delivering various Super Rich Solutions (see Exhibit 6.4).

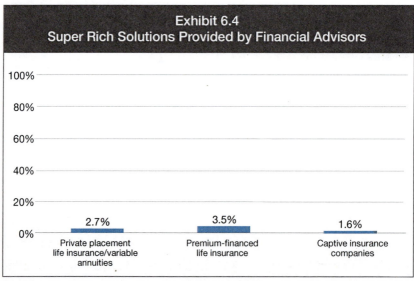

N = 803 wealth managers. Source: Russ Alan Prince and John J. Bowen Jr., *Becoming Seriously Wealthy: How to Harness the Strategies of the Super Rich and Ultra-Wealthy Business Owners*, 2017.

One of the largest opportunities for private client lawyers among the wealthy and even more so among the ultra-wealthy and Super Rich is their interest in private placement life insurance and private placement variable annuities. Private client lawyers familiar with the nature and applications of these high-end wealth management products are better positioned to work with the very wealthy, as well as with many higher-end financial advisors.

Because of their understanding and proficiency with private placement life insurance and private placement variable annuities, they are increasingly likely to be brought into high-net-worth client situations by financial advisors who can deliver the products but do not see all the ramifications and high-net-worth client possibilities.

For example, the ability to use private placement variable annuities in conjunction with a charitable trust can enable successful business owners to create what are often called charitable retirement plans. And there is strong demand for charitable retirement plans from philanthropically motivated entrepreneurs.

Another sizable opportunity for many private client lawyers is facilitating premium-financed life insurance transactions in the context of estate planning or deferred compensation plans. Private client lawyers are not expected to be the technical experts when it comes to this product. On the other hand, by understanding the pros and cons and—more important—the versatility of premium-financed life insurance in an estate or deferred compensation plan, private client lawyers can play an instrumental role in facilitating the delivery of the wealth management product and be compensated for their planning expertise.

There are quite a few additional wealth management products in which private client lawyers can play a strong role and be well-compensated. Another example is captive insurance companies. There is a vast opportunity for captive insurance companies because relatively few businesses are using them, and they can often prove very beneficial. Here, private client lawyers can have extensive involvement, resulting in both value-based project fees and retainer fees, thereby generating a steady flow of revenue and probably opening the door to a lot of new business.

A related service private client lawyers can provide is opinion letters addressing various wealth management products and transactions. When appropriate, opinion letters insulate high-net-worth clients from certain adverse consequences. The necessity and appropriateness of opinion letters vary depending on the high-net-worth client and the particular situation. Aside from usually being inherently profitable, providing well-reasoned opinion letters can often lead to stronger relationships and the delivery of additional legal services.

The bottom line is that by being knowledgeable about Super Rich Solutions, private client lawyers can both generate substantially more revenue from their own high-net-worth clientele and possibly obtain a very significant amount of new wealthy clients from high-caliber financial advisors. It's important to recognize that private client lawyers are usually not going to be the experts when it comes to the wealth management products. Instead, their contribution is in knowing the role Super Rich Solutions play in helping high-net-worth clients achieve their agendas and in developing and implementing the plans.

Through street-smart networking, which we'll discuss in Chapter 7, private client lawyers can connect with like-minded, noncompeting professionals such as select financial advisors who have a meaningful number of high-net-worth clients. Although there are many ways to create "economic glue" between private client lawyers and financial advisors, the ability to help facilitate Super Rich Solutions is quite powerful.

It's important to realize that facilitating Super Rich Solutions is applicable and easily doable for many smart private client lawyers (even though we do not presently find it all that common). This is a way for you to speedily move along the path to serious wealth.

Addressing the adverse impact of great wealth on the heirs and the family

For many of the wealthy, a major concern is the possible or prevalent adverse impact their personal fortunes have on their families. From the "rich kids of Instagram" who flaunt their wealth on social media to severe abuses by the very wealthy of other people because of an exaggerated sense of entitlement, some to-be heirs are causing tremendous damage to their futures and may be imposing grave hardships on their families.

In these scenarios, private client lawyers unite what the eminent German sociologist Max Weber called opposing "value spheres." For the wealthy family, they combine the rational calculated world with the socio-emotive world, resulting in balanced decisions. It's about getting all the family members aligned—or as aligned as possible.

A large percentage of self-made millionaires, multimillionaires and billionaires are very concerned that their children do not have a sensible perspective on wealth. There are many examples of this, including:

- Purchasing a new Lamborghini every year and trashing the old one to have the latest model.

- When the "child" is 32 years old and his career is shopping for himself.

- Rotating husbands because they get boring after about six months. This involves paying them exorbitantly to "go away."

- When a "vacation" is an extended stay in rehab.

- Buying a 200+ acre horse farm because she wants to learn to ride and then selling the property for half what she paid after discovering horses do not do what they are told.

Dealing with the adverse impact of great wealth on the family is many times increasingly problematic with respect to larger personal fortunes. This is evidenced in our study of 199 single-family offices, where two-thirds of the senior executives in the single-family offices reported that Super Rich families were having troubles because of their children's behavior that was caused by their inability to effectively cope with great wealth (see Exhibit 6.5).

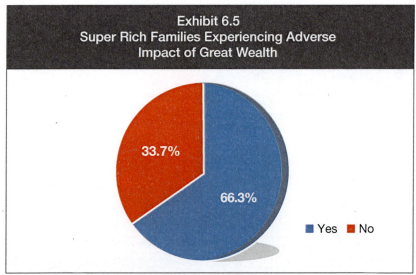

N = 199 senior executives at single-family offices. Source: AES Nation.

This is not necessarily surprising as many of these children grew up in an environment that can foster a skewed perspective on money. We have also found that many times the problems are not caused by the environment in which the children were raised, but by unrelated dysfunction or mental health challenges.

Of course, it's common among all families with children to have problems. When it comes to the Super Rich, the ability to use money as a shield and safety net as well as to exploit the possibilities of great wealth can easily make these children quite difficult to deal with over time. However, this is not a universal condition, as many of the wealthy do not have problems dealing with family money matters.

For those who have such problems, private client lawyers can provide a viable sounding board and set of viewpoints, and can assist in dealing with these and related family problems. Here private client lawyers are helping the wealthy tackle pressing and disturbing tribulations that can badly impact their children and their families.

Being able to help a wealthy family manage unfavorable complications of great wealth is a perfect role for many private client lawyers, as legal issues often dovetail with effective solutions. Examples of legal solutions include:

- **Determining the most appropriate trust arrangements.** This action goes beyond structuring a trust to ensuring that all parties clearly understand the logic and implications of the particular structure.

- **Developing an effective approach to family governance.** This can include documentation that memorializes the values and thinking of the wealthy family, such as a family constitution and family mission statement.

- **Integrating philanthropy into family life in a highly constructive manner.** While the giving entity can be a private foundation, for example, the systematic involvement of family members can facilitate communicating and embodying family values.

- **Acting as mediator among wealthy family members to help resolve intrafamily disputes.** This is a fast-developing technical niche specialty as so many of the wealthy do not want to go to court and potentially open up their lives to public scrutiny.

There are many possibilities for private client lawyers working with high-net-worth families who are having troubles due to being very wealthy. However, less than one in five of the private client lawyers in our study is focused on this matter (see Exhibit 6.6). In contrast, nearly nine out

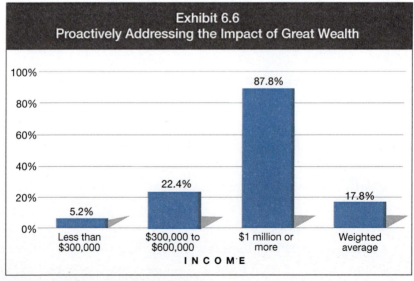

N = 359 private client lawyers. Source: AES Nation.

of ten of the elite private client lawyers were proactively addressing the impact of great wealth with some of their high-net-worth clients.

With the astronomical growth of the number and aggregate wealth of high-net-worth families, coupled with the inherent dysfunction of some families or family members, this area is likely to grow in importance for private client lawyers. What is also very appealing about the area is that it lends itself to value-based project and retainer fees, which we will address in Chapter 11.

The takeaways

To create an exceptional high-net-worth legal practice and potentially build substantial wealth, you have tremendous possibilities in building a profitable clientele with successful business owners and potentially with the Super Rich and single-family offices. At the same time, many other types of wealthy clients can be very rewarding. We very briefly examined a few of them. Each of these types of high-net-worth clients has multiplicative law firm implications.

There are other potential growth areas. We looked at two of them: facilitating Super Rich Solutions and helping ultra-wealthy families deal with the adverse impact of great wealth.

In all these situations, it can be very important for high-net-worth clients, prospects and referral sources to know the quality of the private client lawyers they are considering, which brings us to the importance of thought leadership. Before going there, we turn to the most effective ways of sourcing new high-net-worth clients for private client legal services.

PART III

Best Practices for Building an Exceptional High-Net-Worth Practice

Let's say it's a given for private client lawyers to be technically proficient, highly skilled practitioners. The complication is that although being a smart, clever, exceedingly learned professional is critical to doing the very best job for wealthy clients, it is often not enough to build an exceptional high-net-worth legal practice and potentially become seriously wealthy. You almost always need to also effectively implement best practices.

Based on empirical research with diversely successful private client lawyers and other professionals such as multifamily offices, wealth managers and accountants, we have been able to discern an extensive set of best practices that can help transform and even dramatically improve your revenue capability. In this section, we will address five best practices that are regularly instrumental in building an exceptional high-net-worth legal practice.

It's critical for you not just to understand the nature and applicability of the various best practices, but also to commit to making them an integral part of your law firm. You need to both know what works *and* put that knowledge to work.

CHAPTER 7

Source Wealthy Clients from Noncompeting Professionals

The most technically brilliant private client lawyer is worthless, from a revenue-generating perspective, without clients. The ability to source wealthy clients on preferential terms is central to creating and growing an exceptional high-net-worth legal practice that can be the foundation for serious wealth.

With the increasing commoditization of legal services, more intense competition and increasingly cost-sensitive high-net-worth clients, rainmaking is a cornerstone of significant professional success. And as we noted in Chapter 2, sourcing high-quality wealthy clients is a major concern of more than four out of five of the private client lawyers surveyed. Without question, your ability to bring in new wealthy and—better yet, Super Rich clients—is one of your more demanding tasks as a private client lawyer.

There are many ways to source high-net-worth clients. Some are unquestionably more powerful than others. We will begin by delineating how private client lawyers get *most* of their new clients. Then we will turn to how they get their best high-net-worth clients.

The *most* clients

We can evaluate the effectiveness and efficiency of business development methodologies in several ways. Two principal considerations are how private client lawyers get *most* of their wealthy clients and how they get their *best* clients.

Over the previous three years, about 70 percent of the private client lawyers surveyed had sourced most of their high-net-worth clients from their current high-net-worth clients (see Exhibit 7.1). This is particularly the case for those private client lawyers earning less than $600,000 annually. Referrals from satisfied wealthy clients have commonly been the way most private client lawyers and other professionals obtain wealthy clients.

Exhibit 7.1
Sourcing the Majority of Their Wealthy Clients
(previous three years)

Source	INCOME			
	Less than $300,000	$300,000 to $600,000	$1 million or more	Weighted average
Clients	78.9%	62.7%	14.6%	68.5%
Noncompeting professionals	6.0%	14.9%	75.6%	15.6%
Personal contacts	7.6%	13.4%	0.0%	7.8%
Third-party events	3.2%	4.5%	9.8%	4.2%
Firm-organized events	1.6%	3.0%	0.0%	1.7%
Other	2.7%	1.5%	0.0%	2.2%

N = 359 private client lawyers. Source: AES Nation.

Client referrals are predominately a function of two factors. The first is the quality of expertise private client lawyers provide. The second is whether the wealthy client was asked by another person whom they use for legal services, and to a lesser degree, for an introduction to that lawyer. When it comes to client referrals, the wealthy clients drive the process, not the private client lawyers.

Referrals from other noncompeting professionals are the second-most important source of wealthy clients overall. (These other professionals range from lawyers with other specialties such as commercial and matrimonial services to different types of professionals working with high-net-worth clients, such as wealth managers, accountants, life insurance professionals, high-end personal lines specialists and financial advisors in multifamily offices.)

For about a sixth of those surveyed, these referrals resulted in most of their new wealthy clients. This is the case for 6 percent of those earning the lowest annual incomes, rising to about 22 percent for those earning between $300,000 and $600,000. In contrast, three-quarters of the elite private client lawyers are getting most of their wealthy clients from introductions made by noncompeting professionals.

Each of the other sources of potential new high-net-worth clients we evaluated accounts for a much smaller proportion of new wealthy clients. Personal contacts are people (not professionals working with the wealthy) the private client lawyers know. Third-party events are conferences, workshops and symposiums where the private client lawyer is presenting. Firm-organized events are venues for the private client lawyers that they arranged. Lastly, "other" is everything else, including internet marketing efforts.

While client referrals are the biggest source of new wealthy clients for most private client lawyers, it's not the way they get their *best* clients.

The *best* clients

When it comes to accessing the best high-net-worth clients, the most effective source is noncompeting professionals (see Exhibit 7.2). Keep in mind that a dense network of professional advisors supports the requirements and aims of the wealthy. In addition to lawyers, they engage accountants, wealth managers, private bankers, philanthropic specialists, concierge health care providers and family security specialists, among others. By constructively and systematically tapping into these networks, you can conceivably access wealthy clients.

Exhibit 7.2
Sourcing Their Best Wealthy Clients (previous three years)

Source	INCOME			
	Less than $300,000	$300,000 to $600,000	$1 million or more	Weighted average
Noncompeting professionals	61.4%	73.1%	95.2%	67.4%
Clients	33.1%	20.9%	2.4%	27.3%
Personal contacts	3.6%	4.5%	0.0%	3.3%
Third-party events	0.8%	1.5%	2.4%	1.1%
Other	0.8%	0.0%	0.0%	0.6%
Firm-organized events	0.4%	0.0%	0.0%	0.3%

N = 359 private client lawyers. Source: AES Nation.

A very pronounced pattern can be seen among the private client lawyers we surveyed. The more monetarily successful they are, the more they have obtained their best clients from noncompeting professionals over the last three years.

It's notable in the private wealth industry that as professionals concentrate on working with wealthier and wealthier clients, these clients are increasingly *less* inclined to refer their moneyed peers. Billionaires, for example, tend not to be big on sharing with others the professionals in whom they have a great deal of faith and confidence. This is not only characteristic of billionaires; sharing professionals—for many reasons, some logical and some less so—tends to generally be anathema to wealthy and ultra-wealthy individuals. Consequently, the optimal way to source the wealthy, especially the exceptionally wealthy, is by obtaining high-caliber referrals from noncompeting professionals.

Before turning to how to most effectively garner referrals from other types of noncompeting professionals, it's useful to recognize that you can directly cultivate high-net-worth clients. There is considerable evidence that going direct in a methodical and very process-oriented way can be very worthwhile in sourcing wealthy clients.

The direct approach

Undeniably, referrals—particularly referrals from noncompeting professionals—are usually the optimal way to source high-net-worth clients. Still, in our experience, some private client lawyers who have taken a direct approach have achieved great success.

Presenting at CEO forums and corporate-focused mastermind groups, for example, can open the door to successful, affluent business owners. Examples of these organizations include:

- **Vistage International.** Membership is business owners and C-level executives who meet in small groups to work though issues.

- **Young Presidents' Organization (YPO).** A global network of business leaders connecting to learn and share ideas for personal and professional growth.

- **CEO Roundtable.** Business owners are brought together regularly to exchange ideas and insights.

There are also chambers of commerce and the multitude of events produced for business owners. All in all, there are many organizations and associations that can provide you with direct access to successful business owners. There are also other types of groups for other types of prospective high-net-worth clients.

Another example of going direct with the aim of sourcing some of the highest of high-net-worth clients is coordinating or being involved in single-family office symposiums. The people running and owning single-family offices are often looking for answers that translate into solid results. While they are attracted to a wide array of events, many of these conferences fall short on delivering value—a fact that has become quite evident to this growing community.

The professionalization of the single-family office industry is leading to new ways for those in charge to share and learn. One approach getting a lot of play is commonly called "doing lunch." Here, a handful of single-family office executives and often Super Rich family members meet over an extended lunch to focus on a carefully crafted agenda that covers one or two items where concrete next steps are delineated.

Along the same line, a growing number of senior executives and Super Rich family members have determined that symposiums are an excellent way to begin to learn about and in some cases master capabilities that can significantly improve the performance of their single-family office. Clearly, it's critical to use the proven pedagogical methodologies that make symposiums exceptionally successful. Otherwise these experiences can be very unsatisfying.

At a symposium, the senior executives of a single-family office and ultra-wealthy family members are looking for in-depth conversations and an open sharing of ideas, concepts and experiences, as opposed to lectures—especially canned presentations. The intent of a symposium is to foster thought-provoking educational experiences so the attendees leave with actionable solutions. To make symposiums successful for you as a private client lawyer requires communicating your expertise in a usable manner—something that can be quite a feat, considering the often-complex nature of the subject matter.

You can readily run such events on your own or in conjunction with noncompeting professionals. You can also be an expert participant at symposiums. From these assemblies, you can start dialogs with the Super Rich or senior executives attending. This can put you squarely in the selection set when there is a need for legal expertise.

While these presentations for successful business owners, "doing lunch" and single-family office symposiums can be very useful, still the most pervasively powerful way of sourcing wealthy clients remains referrals from noncompeting professionals.

The rationale for focusing on sourcing high-net-worth clients from noncompeting professionals

There are two interrelated reasons referrals from noncompeting professionals are so effective in enabling private client lawyers to build exceptional high-net-worth legal practices: access and powerful introductions.

When the wealthy get together, there is a strong likelihood they are not discussing legal services and providers. More often they are talking about their businesses and the stresses they are under because of their businesses. They also discuss, within limits, their personal lives such as the grandchildren or the new spouse. To a small degree, usually when prompted by the other party, the wealthy will discuss professional services, including legal services. They might even mention the experts they engage.

While there are creative and formidable ways to facilitate referrals from existing clients (affluent and not), the access many of these clients have to the wealthy is probably restrained because:

- **High-net-worth clients know relatively few wealthy people.** Most very wealthy people do not necessarily spend a great deal of their time—business or personal—with other very wealthy people. This is even more the case as they move up the net worth spectrum.

- **High-net-worth clients do not see many opportunities to refer.** Most wealthy clients do not typically find "appropriate" situations to suggest private client lawyers to their peers. From not being able to adequately explain private client legal services to being uncomfortable recommending professionals (a common phenomenon), wealthy clients are often not inclined to make introductions.

- **High-net-worth clients are often unable to screen for qualified referrals.** It is very common for wealthy client referrals to be inappropriate. This has a lot to do with their inability to accurately qualify the people they are trying to refer.

These challenges are easily sidestepped when working with noncompeting professionals. Experts in related fields can make powerful introductions to you because they are:

- **Validating your expertise.** The noncompeting professionals are saying you are one of the very best professionals for the job. It's optimal if the noncompeting professional can concurrently provide a rationale and supporting materials that demonstrate your capabilities and talents, such as evidence that you are a thought leader.

- **Emphasizing a personal fit.** The noncompeting professional is saying you will have good rapport with the wealthy client. The emphasis is that not only can you do a great job, but you are also a good person to do business with and the wealthy individual or family will like you.

- **Providing impetus to action.** The noncompeting professional is, in effect, saying to the wealthy client, "You need this lawyer's expertise, and you need it now." This is a matter of highlighting the importance of engaging you promptly, as procrastinating will only be detrimental. Very often, the noncompeting professional is providing a formidable call to action.

In these situations, the hard-earned, high-quality business and personal relationships noncompeting professionals share with their wealthy clients are to varying degrees transferred to you, the private client lawyer. To make this happen consistently, you must create strategic partnerships.

The advantage of strategic partnerships

Strategic partnerships are a special type of relationship between professionals. As Exhibit 7.3 shows, they are dramatically different from *strategic relationships*.

Exhibit 7.3 Strategic Relationships Compared to Strategic Partnerships	
Strategic relationships	**Strategic partnerships**
Periodically a wealthy client is pointed in the private client lawyer's direction.	On a regular basis, the noncompeting professional introduces the private client lawyer to his or her wealthy clients and actively lobbies on his or her behalf.
The private client lawyer is one of several lawyers being considered.	The private client lawyer is the only or primary lawyer for the noncompeting professional's wealthy clients.
Most of the opportunities are driven by the wealthy clients as opposed to the noncompeting professional.	The noncompeting professional is vigorously looking to make strong introductions of his or her wealthy clients to the private client lawyer.

Strategic relationships will possibly refer a new wealthy client to you now and again. When they do make these referrals, you should not be surprised to be one of several lawyers the professional is naming for the wealthy client to consider. What is most telling in these situations is that it is the wealthy client who usually prompts the other professional to make a referral.

In contrast, strategic partnerships support you directly. These noncompeting professionals are exceedingly proactive in finding wealthy clients for you. And when they share their wealthy clients with you, they are not even considering other lawyers.

Clearly, strategic partnerships are the intended result of connecting with noncompeting professionals with the aim of garnering new high-net-worth clients. By evaluating the way elite professionals with differing expertise accomplish this, we systematized the process. We call it street-smart networking.

The street-smart networking process

To source the best high-net-worth clients, you would be well-advised to create strategic partnerships with noncompeting professionals who have wealthy clients. A proven systematic process to facilitate strategic partnerships is street-smart networking.

Street smarts largely define many of the most financially accomplished professionals working with the wealthy. Street-smart networking is the methodology used by tremendously successful professionals to connect with other professionals, resulting in a steady stream of new high-net-worth clients. These actions are key to the approach:

- **Set high, but grounded aspirations.** Street-smart networking starts with your aspirations. Having notable and often lofty goals tends to foster a virtuous cycle of motivation and actions. It also sets the baseline for measuring your success and enabling refinement.

- **Advance the agenda.** With your goals in place, preparation is essential. You need to put together a plan. Very successful professionals are quite good at determining what it will take to achieve their high, but grounded, aspirations. They often develop an understanding by being astute, lifelong learners coupled with being constructively self-critical.

- **Conduct assessments.** The ability to ably evaluate noncompeting professionals is at the very core of extraordinary networking success. This involves making extreme efforts to develop a broad and deep understanding of the noncompeting professionals you are connecting with. Central to these assessments are three core questions, described below.

- **Ensure alignment.** You must effectively align interests between yourself and the noncompeting professional. To do this, you need street smarts. Aligning your interests is usually based first on a deep understanding of the noncompeting professional's critical concerns and second on his or her expressed intent.

- **Measure achievements.** To get optimal results, you must make sure you are on track. This entails regularly comparing your results to your aspirations. When there is a disconnect, make the requisite adjustments.

Street-smart networking is a highly systematic and thoughtful framework for identifying and working with others—in this case noncompeting professionals—to achieve significant results. It is a mindful and exacting set of means that fosters intense success and regularly opens up considerable new business possibilities.

Three core questions of street-smart networking

As we have discussed, there are a number of aspects to your ability to effectively network with noncompeting professionals to source high-net-worth clients. To establish strategic partnerships, you need to be able to answer these three questions:

- **Who can help you achieve your goals?** When you know what you want to accomplish, you will be better able to triage the many noncompeting professionals you meet to determine which prospective relationships can be most useful. At the same time, you will be able to proactively identify those noncompeting professionals who will likely prove most valuable, as well as those who are not likely to be fruitful.

- **What do the noncompeting professionals care about?** Knowing what you want to accomplish and even knowing whom to talk to are often the easy parts. You also need to identify the critical motivations and dominant preferences of the noncompeting professionals.

- **How are you going to get the noncompeting professionals to care about you achieving your goals?** When you can connect what they care about to your agenda, you will be able to motivate them to introduce you to their wealthy clients on a consistent basis. More often than not, you will need "economic glue"—direct and indirect financial incentives that motivate each partner to work on behalf of the other to further their mutual success.

Being able to accurately answer these questions has been shown to be transformational for many private client lawyers, commonly resulting in new and wealthier clients. Your answers may periodically change with your circumstances, but the value of thinking strategically will likely make monumental differences in your ability to get results when networking with noncompeting professionals.

The takeaways

Referrals from satisfied clients are the way most private client lawyers source most of their new clients. However, referrals from noncompeting professionals turn out to be the way they predominantly obtain their best wealthy clients. Although there are ways private client lawyers can go directly to prospective high-net-worth clients, being introduced to the wealthy by noncompeting professionals will likely continue to be the optimal approach for sourcing new and wealthier high-net-worth clients.

You can therefore accelerate your success by employing systematic processes such as street-smart networking to create strategic partnerships. Your aim is to create a pipeline—a steady stream of new high-net-worth clients.

Being a thought leader is instrumental to supporting all your high-net-worth business development efforts. We turn to that topic next.

CHAPTER 8

Benefit from Being a Thought Leader

Being a thought leader has been empirically shown to translate into higher revenue for almost any client-facing professional. Furthermore, the professionals who work with the wealthy know the value of thought leadership. The complication is that there are very few true thought leaders—although many professionals aspire to the title.

When private client lawyers, or any other professionals for that matter, call themselves thought leaders, there is a strong possibility they are not. For example, a "Thought Leadership" tab on a website rarely converts into being perceived as a thought leader. When professionals proclaim themselves thought leaders, a fair number of them are not really garnering the benefits of being a thought leader.

In contrast, when other professionals, high-net-worth clients and the media say a private client lawyer is a thought leader, then he or she probably is a thought leader and is likely accruing enormous business advantages.

What is a thought leader?

With so many professionals bandying around the term "thought leader," it's worthwhile to clearly define the concept.

There are many definitions of the term "thought leader." Some people take a very expansive view of the term, wrapping internal strategy and corporate culture into their definition. Other pundits are more constrained in their definition.

The way we define thought leadership emphasizes the potential exponential business rewards of being a thought leader. Hence, you can't be a thought leader unless you are capitalizing on the dramatically enhanced brand equity you will attain by the stature conveyed by being a thought leader.

Based on decades of working with elite professionals, their firms and other types of organizations, we use a two-part definition of what constitutes a thought leader:

- **Definition (part one).** *A thought leader is an individual or firm that prospects, clients, referral sources, intermediaries and even competitors recognize as one of the foremost authorities in selected areas of specialization, resulting in being the go-to individual or organization for said expertise.*

Brilliance is a function of acclaim, created where others bestow the accolades. Consequently, others anoint private client lawyers as thought leaders. We now move to the second part of the definition, the commercial component:

- **Definition (part two).** *A thought leader is an individual or firm that significantly profits from being recognized as such.*

It's probably fair to say that, by and large, you are in business to make money. You want to do a top-notch job for your clients, but no doubt you want to be well-compensated to the extent possible. Being a thought leader is very much about making money—thereby contributing to the goal of building serious wealth.

To become a thought leader, it's especially critical that you monetize your state-of-the-art thinking by increasing your ability to source, work with and profit from wealthy clients. In effect, being a thought leader requires the ability to garner radically above-average returns for your investment and effort required to become a thought leader.

The importance of being a thought leader

Thought leadership is a very viable and often even essential component of creating the exceptional high-net-worth legal practice that can be your foundation for serious wealth. There are extensive business benefits to being a thought leader, including the ability to retain wealthy clients over extended time periods and generate new engagements from them.

Being a thought leader can also be a very powerful way to facilitate getting high-net-worth referrals—especially from noncompeting professionals. You can even use intellectual capital as a means of "compensating" non-competing professionals for making high-net-worth client referrals.

Being a thought leader is a form of reputational capital. Several factors are often critical when wealthy prospects choose their private client lawyers, including:

- The more complicated and involved the offerings, the more the wealthy are disposed to turn to recognized state-of-the-art private client legal authorities—thought leaders.

- The harder it is to directly evaluate and compare legal strategies (which is usually the case), the more appealing thought leaders become.

- The more detrimental and potentially adverse the consequences of choosing the wrong private client lawyer can be, the more effort the wealthy will put into finding who they would define as the best—and the best are often thought leaders.

As we saw in the previous chapter, referrals from noncompeting professionals are often the optimal way to source new high-net-worth clients. This is even more the case as the level of wealth increases. However, for the referral source—a wealth manager, for instance—making such introductions can be a high-risk endeavor.

If the referral does not work out well, the credibility and judgment of the referral source come into question. Because professional services are all about credibility and judgment, the referral source—the wealth manager in our example—can end up being a very big loser. Making an introduction to a thought leader goes a long way toward mitigating the risk.

Because of the potential for damage to their own reputations, many noncompeting professionals are reticent about making referrals to private client lawyers. Thought leadership makes it easier for noncompeting professionals to refer their high-net-worth clients to a particular private client lawyer for these reasons:

- **Validates the private client lawyer's expertise.** The fact that noncompeting professionals can point to a private client lawyer's stature and standing as a thought leader enables them to comfortably and actively recommend his or her legal services to their wealthy clients with greater confidence and legitimacy.

- **More easily communicates the private client lawyer's expertise.** When making introductions, it is common for the noncompeting professional to not be very practiced at making the case for private client legal services. When the referral source can mention the thought leadership content of the private client lawyer, that can be very helpful in eliminating this problem.

- **Acts as currency for qualified introductions.** The thought leadership content that helps noncompeting professionals become more successful is a very powerful form of currency. This motivates them to proactively identify and introduce their wealthy clients to private client lawyers who are providing this information and insights.

The advantages of being a thought leader are not lost on the private client lawyers we surveyed, as about three-quarters of them say being a recognized legal authority is very important to business development (see Exhibit 8.1). This perspective proportionately increases with the income of the private client lawyer.

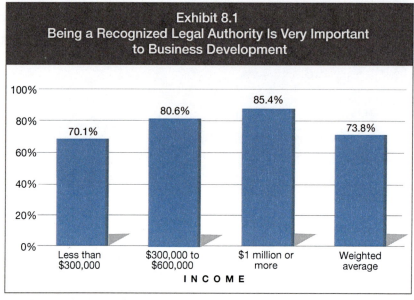

N = 359 private client lawyers. Source: AES Nation.

Although many private client lawyers understand the power of being a thought leader, only a quarter of them are actively working on being recognized legal authorities (see Exhibit 8.2). There is an even more dramatic differential in favor of the higher-earning private client lawyers.

We hear many reasons from private client lawyers about why they do not actively work on becoming thought leaders. The two biggest obstacles are a lack of time and a lack of knowledge about becoming a thought leader.

Scarcity of time is endemic for most successful professionals working with high-net-worth clients, and striving to become a thought leader is a time-intense endeavor. Nevertheless, if you make the time and put in the effort, becoming a thought leader will likely be very rewarding.

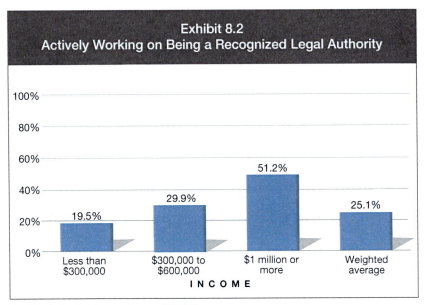

N = 359 private client lawyers. Source: AES Nation.

The other major obstacle is a lack of knowledge about how to become a thought leader. Becoming a thought leader—provided you are indeed a legal expert—is actually a fairly mechanical process.

The two components of powerful thought leadership

At this point, it's important to understand the two core components to becoming a thought leader:

- You must be an expert.

- You must have high-value content—intellectual capital—you want to share.

The information and insights you provide should both resonate with your intended audience and say something that can make a meaningful difference in their lives.

With the relative ease of conducting primary research and the drive among many professionals to become thought leaders and work with the wealthy, an overflow of content is being developed that addresses the world of the wealthy. In fact, there is a deluge of content that—more often than not—creates a fog of confusion.

All this content results in a great deal of thought *followship*, not thought *leadership*. Instead of cutting-edge assessments, thinking and solutions, there is too much repetition of basic ideas and concepts, dated trends and random benchmarking.

A dull recycling of established strategies and perceptions of the wealthy will not help you become a thought leader. You need perspectives, insights, actions and solutions that can make important differences for your intended audience.

Understanding the offerings of your competitors can help you produce distinctive, higher-quality content. You can differentiate your content from that of competitors in several strategic ways:

- **The step strategy.** Leverage the intellectual capital of your competitors. The result will be an incremental but meaningful improvement on what is currently available.

- **The superiority strategy.** Go head-to-head with your competitors based on the same or very similar intellectual capital. Your goal would be to deliver a considerably better set of solutions and/or a superior experience. The winner is the professional who implements most effectively.

- **The innovation strategy.** Avoid any conflicts or perceptual positioning overlaps, and develop intellectual capital that is innovative and applicable—and consequently appealing to the wealthy and meaningful referral sources.

It's useful to evaluate what your competitors are doing with respect to thought leadership. However, keep in mind that it's a very big world and being the first mover can give you a major strategic advantage.

Distributing your thought leadership content

Developing exceptional thought leadership content will enable you to gain a key differential advantage. However, it will all be for naught if your sensational thought leadership content fails to reach your intended audiences: the wealthy and/or strong potential referral sources.

When contemplating distribution channels, your first consideration should be how to structure and communicate your thought leadership content. Examples of this include:

- **Packaged content.** Making thought leadership content tangible has historically been achieved and is still accomplished by packaging it into bylined articles, law firm-produced reports, podcasts, books and the like.

- **Live events.** To succeed in business development, it is often critical to "press the flesh." Optimally, your goal is one-to-one (also team-to-team) meetings. However, a solid intermediary step and a very potent way to communicate exceptional thought leadership content is by participating in events such as conferences, workshops and symposiums.

- **Social media.** Where your communications are web-based and mobile, and you want to create a community of like-minded individuals, we have the fast-changing and potentially confusing world of social media. Bear in mind that there are many different forms of social media such as forums, blogs, wikis and community networking sites. To date, social media, while potentially effective in connecting with noncompeting professionals who can refer their high-net-worth clients, has proven of limited value to private client lawyers in connecting directly with the wealthy.

Effective thought leadership content distribution is more arduous than ever, particularly when it comes to reaching the wealthy and the very wealthy. Aside from leveraging their circle of contacts (including social media connections), most private client lawyers have very limited reach. Nevertheless, you can expand your reach in many ways. One way, for example, is to present at third-party events where someone else has put the intended audience—successful business owners, for example—in the room.

Thought leadership done badly

Becoming a thought leader will bring you scores of benefits, but there is a downside if you get it wrong. That downside can prove quite painful, if not brutal. You can find yourself in one of three categories if your thought leadership initiatives are done poorly:

- **Invisibles.** The best-case scenario of doing a poor job at becoming a thought leader is that the private client lawyer experiences no repercussions from his or her high-net-worth clients and referral sources. In these circumstances, all the time spent, effort expended and money invested are just written off. However, when private client lawyers execute thought leadership activities badly, the best-case scenario is not always what happens.

- **Benchwarmers.** When thought leadership efforts falter, the consequences can be the reverse of what was intended. Instead of being seen as talented experts, the private client lawyers convey that their understanding of critical industry issues is superficial at best, or that their legal solutions are anything but. A badly conceived or executed thought leadership endeavor easily conveys that the private client lawyer belongs in the minor leagues, warming the bench or just carrying the water, as opposed to playing on the all-star team.

- **Radioactives.** Even more detrimental is the "reverse halo" effect, where a poor attempt at becoming a thought leader actually diminishes the private client lawyer's offerings in the eyes of the wealthy and referral sources.

These possible adverse consequences do not mean you should abandon the idea of becoming a thought leader. In fact, not making the effort to become a thought leader can be disastrous in these turbulent times.

It's critical to remember that the benefits of being a thought leader are astounding. But approach becoming a thought leader judiciously and prudently. Your decision to become a thought leader must be made very carefully and methodically. Think through what you want to accomplish and how becoming a leading industry authority will achieve these goals.

The takeaways

Being a thought leader can be an excellent and powerful way to boost your ability to source high-net-worth clients—especially very wealthy and successful business owners, as well as the Super Rich and single-family offices. This fact is not lost on most private client lawyers. The complication is that a substantial percentage of private client lawyers are not taking the steps to communicate that they are indeed highly talented and skilled legal practitioners with worthwhile views and advice.

Private client lawyers do not focus on becoming thought leaders for many reasons, including time constraints and concerns about doing it badly. In our experience, for many private client lawyers the biggest obstacle to becoming thought leaders is a lack of knowledge of the methodologies that translate into becoming thought leaders—an obstacle that can be easily overcome.

Because it is hard to access the wealthy and make them clients, it's good business to maximize your existing relationships with these individuals. That is the topic of our next chapter.

CHAPTER 9

Maximize High-Net-Worth Client Relationships

Finding a successful, wealthy business owner and converting him or her into a client is usually a considerable task. Even when you create strategic partnerships with noncompeting professionals, you can put a lot of time and energy into maintaining and enhancing those relationships—and even then, high-net-worth clients still need to be motivated to engage you.

It therefore makes good business sense, once you have new high-net-worth clients, to maximize the legal services you provide to them. This is not only potentially very beneficial to your wealthy clients, but it helps you on the path to serious wealth.

In many ways, maximizing wealthy client relationships is like picking low-hanging fruit. Provided you are delivering outstanding value to your high-net-worth clients, more than likely they will use additional legal services as needed. If you facilitate this process, all involved will benefit. Although this makes a great deal of sense, relatively few private client lawyers are operating this way.

Low-hanging fruit

The term "low-hanging fruit" refers to easily obtainable gains. It's a metaphor for pursuing the simplest and easiest path to results. Where does fruit hang lowest? The answer lies in your own high-net-worth clientele.

In certain transactional situations, there may be no opportunities to provide additional legal services to current wealthy clients. But sometimes private client lawyers fail to maximize their high-net-worth relationships because they discount the possibility of new business from their existing wealthy clients. They believe they have addressed everything needing to be addressed, or they think they have already obtained all the legal work possible.

In our experience, a large percentage of private client lawyers are reticent about looking for additional legal business unless the high-net-worth client has clearly expressed a need for additional legal services. While it indeed is the case that sometimes no further legal services are required, extensive studies with the wealthy over decades have consistently shown this to be an often-inaccurate perception. Because the wealthy are not asking for more legal expertise, that does not mean they would not benefit from more legal expertise.

The key to getting the low-hanging fruit is to have a broad and deep understanding of your high-net-worth clients. First, we will show the financial advantage of being *comprehensive*. Then we will address one time-tested, empirically verified effective way to understand the wealthy: employing a high-net-worth client evaluative methodology known as the Total Client Model.

Comprehensive private client lawyers earn more

In our survey of private client lawyers, we were able to statistically divide them into two segments (see Exhibit 9.1):

- **Comprehensive.** Private client lawyers directly deliver their own expertise and indirectly deliver additional legal services by regularly bringing in other types of lawyers.

- **Limited.** Private client lawyers, for the most part, deliver only their own expertise.

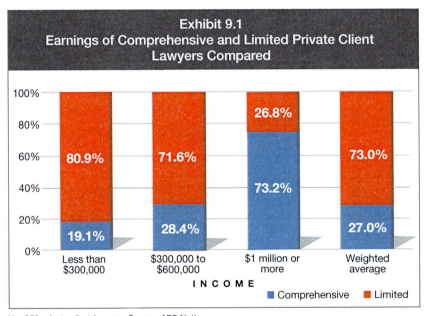

N = 359 private client lawyers. Source: AES Nation.

Overall, 27 percent of private client lawyers are *comprehensive,* while the remaining 73 percent are *limited.* As private client lawyers earn more, they distinctly shift from *limited* to *comprehensive.* Being *comprehensive*

107

probably results from a combination of working with higher-net-worth clients who have more complex situations and being proactive in identifying and capitalizing on other legal needs and wants.

The difference between the two types of private client lawyers is the number of diverse legal services being provided to a single high-net-worth client. The greater the number of diverse legal services, the more profitable wealthy clients are for private client lawyers. The ability to be *comprehensive*, coupled with working with wealthier clients, is essential to creating an exceptional high-net-worth legal practice and, consequently, to building serious wealth.

This logic supports the fact that so many private client lawyers identify successful business owners and their companies as highly preferred clients. Not only do these clients have significant personal legal needs and wants, but their companies also make use of extensive legal services. Furthermore, the relative complexity of their situations means that the legal solutions are often not cookie-cutter. The same rationale is even more applicable to the Super Rich and single-family offices, as well as to many other types of high-net-worth clients.

To be *comprehensive*, you need a network of other types of lawyers. This is not the stumbling block, as just about all those surveyed know capable lawyers in other fields to whom they would refer their high-net-worth clients when appropriate (see Exhibit 9.2).

The problem in delivering a diverse range of legal and related services is usually proactively identifying the opportunities for more legal services. These opportunities can be for more legal expertise provided by you or for the expertise of other types of lawyers you can refer to the wealthy client.

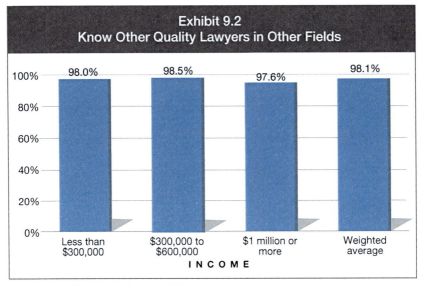

N = 359 private client lawyers. Source: AES Nation.

This is an all too common conundrum among all the professionals working with the wealthy. Wealth managers, accountants, private bankers and so forth are generally unable to determine additional ways they can provide their expertise or the knowledge and skills of other professionals to their wealthy clients. An effective solution is to employ the Total Client Model.

The Total Client Model

It's not possible for you to learn too much about your high-net-worth clients. The more you know about your wealthy clients, the better you can serve them. We have tapped the experience and know-how of elite professionals who have large numbers of extremely satisfied extremely wealthy clients to develop a framework for information gathering that will enable you to assess client needs, wants, preferences and—very importantly—opportunities.

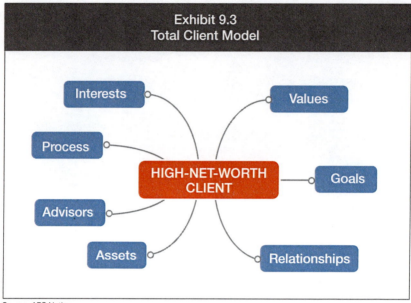

Source: AES Nation.

The framework we devised is called the Total Client Model. It is composed of eight categories. The following are sample questions for each category (see Exhibit 9.3):

The high-net-worth client

- What is the client's age?

- What is the client's net worth and average annual income?

- What is the client's high-net-worth personality? (see next chapter)

Values

- What social issues are very important to the client?

- What is the client's religious orientation (and how devout is he or she)?

- What specific values does the client feel are important to communicate to heirs?

Goals

- What are the client's personal and professional goals?

- What does the client want or feel obligated to do for his or her children, other family members, friends, society and the world at large?

- What are the client's aspirations for loved ones?

Relationships

- What family relationships (with a spouse, children, siblings, parents, etc.) are the most important ones in the client's personal and professional life?

- Who are the client's business associates and how important are they?

- What particularly strong business relationships does the client have?

Assets

- How are the client's assets structured?

- How is the client managing financial assets?

- How does the client make money today (and how is that likely to change in the next three years)?

Advisors

- Who are the other advisors the client is using and what role does each advisor play?

- Of late, how frequently has the client switched advisors?

- Which advisors are especially close to the client?

Process

- Who else should be in the room when presenting legal strategies to the client?

- What security measures are being used to protect personal and financial information?

- How detailed should the explanation of legal strategies be when presented to the client?

Interests

- What are the client's favorite activities, TV programs, movies and sports teams?

- Are health and fitness important to the client (and, if so, what is his or her regimen)?
- What charities are important to the client?

The Total Client Model is illustrated as sets of questions. However, we do not advise that you ask all these questions directly. The more effective approach is to make open-ended queries during a careful and systematic discovery process. As you collect information, you can fill in the answers to the extensive sets of questions in each category.

The Total Client Model is being used successfully by all types of professionals working with the wealthy. We have coached private client lawyers, wealth managers, accountants, financial advisors, private bankers, consultants and life insurance agents on how to use it. The framework enables these professionals to obtain a deep understanding of their high-net-worth clients. By knowing the possibilities presented by different fact patterns, you will very likely uncover more opportunities to create high levels of wealthy client satisfaction and generate more business.

Common mistakes to avoid

With commitment and practice, you can become proficient at using the Total Client Model. To help speed that process along, we have identified the most common mistakes to avoid:

- **Focusing intensely on your specialties.** You are well-served by thinking beyond your own legal expertise. The better you can recognize opportunities that cannot be solved exclusively by your services, the better for you and for your high-net-worth clients. Moreover, being able to identify issues and concerns, along with

- **Taking too much for granted.** Many private client lawyers make all sorts of assumptions about their high-net-worth clients. Over time, it's usually a good idea to verify these assumptions, as some of them may be inaccurate. By correcting any impreciseness, you will regularly open the door to new revenue possibilities.

- **Not regularly refining and updating the high-net-worth client's profile.** People's lives are in a perpetual state of flux. While private client lawyers know this to be true, they usually fail to capitalize on it. Review the profiles of your wealthy clients on a regular basis to spot changes and the opportunities they provide.

Client-focused business development plans

By using the Total Client Model, you can frequently get a much better understanding of your wealthy clients and uncover more legal and related business opportunities. But you can supercharge your ability to maximize wealthy client relationships by leveraging the Total Client Model to construct client-focused business development plans.

Many private client lawyers write business development plans. While they certainly can help set the direction and certain activities of a legal practice, they can be limited in delivering substantial results. There are numerous reasons for the limited effectiveness of many business development plans—everything from not being tied to specific anticipated outcomes to being outright shelved soon after they are written.

Instead of creating an overarching business development plan, construct client-focused business development plans using the Total Client Model. For each high-net-worth client you evaluate using the Total Client Model, write a detailed plan for implementing the new legal opportunities you identified. Include here the potential referrals to new wealthy clients. Very simply, client-focused business development plans document the business opportunities you recognized and how you are going to convert these possibilities into deliverables for your high-net-worth clients.

We have found that once private client lawyers become comfortable with creating basic client-focused business development plans, they can "level up." This entails projecting revenue numbers to possible new business, in addition to what they could reasonably earn from sourcing new wealthy clients through client referrals. While these numbers tend to be somewhat off target, they are very often directionally accurate. This permits you to better triage your opportunities.

It's important to remember that client-focused business development plans are always evolving. As you become more and more familiar with the process, you will probably uncover new and creative ways to build your high-net-worth practice. In addition, as your wealthy clients' situations change or external forces impact their lives, you will be better prepared to expeditiously take action that will result in more business.

Staying closely involved

The Total Client Model is a validated framework for understanding a wealthy client's needs, wants, preferences, and financial and life situations. With some practice, you can identify a range of fact patterns that potentially results in new legal and associated business. Once you have identified these opportunities, you must be able to deliver solutions, including ones that involve bringing in other types of lawyers as well as other types of professionals who can deliver the appropriate solutions.

Nearly all private client lawyers know other types of lawyers and other types of professionals such as accountants and wealth managers. However, some make serious mistakes when they introduce other professionals to their high-net-worth clients. It's common for them to simply hand off their wealthy clients to these other professionals. Doing so can shortchange the wealthy client and often negates the ability of private client lawyers to build serious wealth.

A more constructive approach is to remain closely involved. There are two main reasons for this:

1. To make sure your wealthy clients are receiving the best solutions delivered the best ways possible

2. To make sure you are financially benefiting as appropriate

Being closely involved can take several forms, from being entwined in the working arrangements to newer business models such as being a "personal advisor" to the wealthy or creating a law firm-based multifamily office practice.

As a personal advisor, you are the go-to professional for the high-net-worth client. The relationship stays strong; so aside from being the legal authority, you are involved in addressing related business and personal issues.

A more extensive version of the personal advisor is the law firm-based multifamily office practice where a diversity of legal expertise is provided to the wealthy, with the private client lawyer being the professional managing the relationship.

The takeaways

The wealthy tend to have multiple legal issues, which you can address directly or by bringing in other lawyers. However, many times these matters are not recognized or brought up by high-net-worth clients. This means it is up to you to identify and follow through on the issues. Unless you take a holistic approach to understanding your wealthy clients, you are unlikely to see all the possibilities for legal expertise.

The Total Client Model is a validated methodology for gaining the requisite holistic understanding of the wealthy. By skillfully addressing the eight categories, you will be able to develop the foundational perspectives and insights that enable you to connect the dots, commonly resulting in substantial new business.

You also generally need to have other professionals you can access to deal with issues beyond your areas of expertise. It's crucial that you not hand off your wealthy clients to other professionals, as it is often to everyone's advantage that you stay closely involved.

A potentially severe deterrent to success is failing to effectively communicate with your wealthy clients. We address a powerful way to deal with this matter in the next chapter.

CHAPTER 10
Effectively Communicate Legal Strategies

As a professional, your first concern is to serve your wealthy clients to the very best of your abilities. That means doing legal work to the highest standards of the profession. Traditionally, the metric of success has been work executed at an extremely high level of technical proficiency, which unfortunately is rarely understood by the wealthy.

More and more, a complementary idea of quality is emerging. This is the idea of making sure the wealthy understand the *value* of the legal services they are receiving. After all, the best private client legal work in the world is not of much use if the client does not follow through on implementing recommendations.

You have many tools at your disposal to effectively communicate with the wealthy. And the benefits of doing so are considerable:

- Wealthy clients will have ongoing professional relationships for which you are retained as an advisor.

- Wealthy clients may return for additional transactional legal services.

- Wealthy clients, when appropriate, will obtain other types of legal services from you and other lawyers you bring to the table.

- Wealthy clients will recommend you to friends, family members, peers and other advisors they work with.

- Wealthy clients will not avoid telling other high-net-worth individuals to do business with you.

The big problem is that private client lawyers are often not very good at effectively communicating legal strategies.

A failure to communicate

Consider the results of a study of 288 wealthy families (net worth of $10 million or more) who had engaged private client lawyers to design their estate plans, but who never followed through to the end—that is, the wealthy families never signed the documents. These wealthy families gave several different explanations for their decision not to implement their estate plans (see Exhibit 10.1).

Nearly nine out of ten of the wealthy families said that the estate plan did not deal with their goals, wants and objectives. Evidently the professionals involved were unsuccessful in uncovering the "deep issues."

Directly related to this factor is the feeling that their private client lawyers made them uneasy, cited by about 80 percent of the wealthy families. This is an emotional reaction to the private client lawyers not being appropriately empathic and communicating poorly with their wealthy clients.

Just over half of wealthy families thought that their estate plan was too complicated. Of course, estate planning for the wealthy can employ complex and intricate legal strategies. Nevertheless, this finding shows a failure on the part of private client lawyers to get a read on the ability of the high-net-worth client to cope with complexity in the planning.

Evident from this study and others like it is that at times private client lawyers are not always communicating effectively with their high-net-worth clients. While they might be exceptionally technically proficient, failing to effectively communicate with their wealthy clients will usually result in nothing getting done or business getting undone. It will also be a major deterrent to future business.

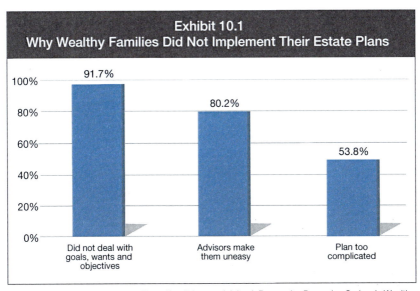

N = 288 wealthy families. Source: Russ Alan Prince and John J. Bowen Jr., *Becoming Seriously Wealthy How to Harness the Strategies of the Super Rich and Ultra-Wealthy Business Owners*, 2017.

A matter of language

As we discussed in Chapter 1, beyond technical proficiencies, effective communication with clients and their other advisors is essential to building an exceptional high-net-worth legal practice. But it's clear that a percentage of private client lawyers fail to communicate well with their wealthy clients. A lot of this has to do with their language.

An intentionally defective trust, for instance, can be a wonderful planning strategy. In our experience, more than a few times, wealthy clients asked for a different trust—one that works; one that is not defective. So why would a private client lawyer discussing freezing the value of a business for estate tax purposes explain to a high-net-worth client that they are going to use an intentionally defective trust? Would it not be so much easier and better for everyone to simply say that they are putting the business into a trust?

Then there are the likes of Rabbi trusts and Crummey powers, which are important but do not necessarily have to be discussed in detail or by name with clients. We were in a meeting with an exceptionally wealthy individual who was completely against using a Rabbi trust. As a Southern Baptist, he wanted a "Minister trust" instead. This request makes perfect sense for this affluent individual. As it turned out, this issue completely derailed the estate planning process and resulted in the firing of the private client lawyer and his law firm, which was handling the client's corporate work.

Our best example is when a multifamily office brought in a truly technically brilliant private client lawyer to talk to one of their Super Rich clients. The astronomically wealthy client was unmarried and without kids, but expected to one day get married and have a family. The prospective client was quite upset after the meeting, resulting in no one getting any business and some bad feelings. It seems that he came away from the meeting believing the private client lawyer was recommending that in the future he could take out a huge life insurance policy on his spouse and that *the spouse could end up floating facedown in the huge swimming pool on his estate.* It's amazing what someone can conclude from the suggestion to have a "floating spouse provision" in an estate plan.

From both experience and the empirical research, it's evident that some private client lawyers are not communicating well with their affluent clients. How, then, can you better communicate legal strategies to your wealthy clients? One very powerful solution is to employ high-net-worth psychology.

High-net-worth psychology

High-net-worth psychology can enable you to better connect with your wealthy clients. The key to better communication of legal solutions is to frame them so you show that you fully understood the needs, wants and goals of the wealthy client and that the legal strategies deliver intended results.

High-net-worth psychology can be exceedingly effective in creating the framework for understanding the specific goals, needs, wants and agendas of wealthy clients. Moreover, high-net-worth psychology is extraordinarily applicable in creating the messaging that drives high-net-worth clients to act.

The high-net-worth psychology framework was developed decades ago using well-established research protocols for creating psychographic segments, or personalities, using surveys of thousands of affluent individuals and multidimensional statistical tools. Since its conception, many elite professionals serving the wealthy—among them private client lawyers, financial advisors in multifamily offices, wealth managers and accountants—have embraced high-net-worth psychology.

These professionals share the need to craft and communicate extremely technical solutions in terms their wealthy clients will understand and value. High-net-worth psychology has been one of the most rigorously tested frameworks in the private wealth industry. Its widespread use is a testament to its reliability and effectiveness. The following is an overview of the nine high-net-worth personalities and some of their key attributes.

Family Stewards

- Want to use their wealth to take care of their family.

- Want to relieve their family members of financial worries.

- Want to fulfill their familial obligations.

Phobics

- Hate being involved in complex decisions.

- Are not at all knowledgeable about legal strategies.

- Dislike discussing technical issues.

Independents

- See attention to legal issues as a necessary evil.
- Want personal freedom.
- Want to have a safety net if they want or need to bail out.

Anonymous

- Confidentiality concerning legal matters is key.
- Secretive about their legal arrangements.
- Extreme privacy is essential for personal comfort.

Moguls

- Worldly success is a way of keeping score and winning.
- Desire considerable power and control over their affairs.
- Seek personal influence.

VIPs

- Success is a way to achieve high status.
- Want to be well-known and respected.
- Seek prestige.

Accumulators

- Their top goal is asset accumulation.

- Want to retain wealth and add to it.

- Their sole objective is to make money.

Gamblers

- Treat dealing with legal matters somewhat as a hobby.

- Derive pleasure from complexity and machinations.

- Relish the problem-solving process.

Innovators

- Perceive legal matters to be an intellectual challenge.

- Want to be on the cutting edge of tax planning.

- Want to employ state-of-the-art wealth management strategies and products.

The *Family Steward* is the most prevalent high-net-worth personality. Family Stewards are motivated by the need to protect their families over the long term. They fear for the safety of their families and are highly motivated to organize defenses against external threats. This motivation makes them excellent candidates for a variety of legal services. When working with Family Stewards, you should demonstrably connect your legal strategy to the need to create long-term protection for the wealthy client and his or her family.

The *Phobic*, the second-most prevalent high-net-worth personality, is typically a wealthy person who dislikes thinking about money and the legal concerns that money brings. Phobics also have significant control issues because they do not think they are capable of effectively managing their own financial and legal affairs. Further, they do not think they are especially capable of effectively managing advisors such as their private client lawyer. When working with a Phobic, it's important to structure simple and clear explanations and to effectively partner with the other trusted advisors to whom they turn for assistance.

Independents are those whose primary objective of accumulating wealth is to achieve financial independence and the accompanying security. Some want to retire from their financial obligations to play golf or go sailing; others will continue to work but value the security of knowing they could leave at any time. You should show Independents how a given legal strategy will foster their goal of personal freedom, and should also communicate your appreciation of their intentions and values.

Anonymous affluent clients are typified by their deep-seated—and sometimes irrational—need for privacy and confidentiality in all their legal and financial affairs. To work effectively with an Anonymous client, you should demonstrate that you diligently protect confidentiality and regularly communicate respect for the high-net-worth client's need for privacy.

Moguls are motivated to accumulate more and more wealth to achieve personal power (and, by extension, influence and control). In short, they want to leverage the power conferred by wealth. You should acknowledge the Mogul's need for control and power and take care to show how any recommended legal strategies will maintain or increase the Mogul's control.

VIPs are motivated to accumulate assets and utilize their wealth to achieve greater status and prestige. VIPs want to be thought well of, especially by other VIPs. They are, as a result, more likely to seek the external symbols of wealth than any other high-net-worth personality. They see such symbols as badges of their exalted status. You should show you understand this need for status and respect and should also relate the wealthy client's situation to similar cases among the "rich and famous" wherever possible.

Accumulators seek to acquire wealth out of an overriding concern for personal financial well-being. Unlike other high-net-worth personalities, Accumulators do not seek to achieve family security or emblems of wealth or power. Instead, their focus is on the continual accumulation and protection of assets as a bulwark against an uncertain future. You should acknowledge your wealthy clients' need for wealth and relate your recommended legal strategies to their need for capital accumulation and protection.

Gamblers believe that their skills and competence will protect them from all significant threats. They view legal and financial affairs as a personal challenge, but one that they are very capable of handling. You can work with this high-net-worth personality effectively if you share nuances of private letter rulings and alternative interpretations of standards. You should also talk with Gamblers about the risks and rewards of alternative legal strategies.

Innovators believe their analytical capabilities will sustain them and protect them from external threats. Because of their lifelong reliance on their analytic capabilities, they are highly self-reliant and do not completely delegate any portion of life tasks having to do with analysis. You should share the details of technical aspects of the legal strategies you recommend and involve them in the heady technical details.

Using high-net-worth psychology to communicate legal strategies

By capitalizing on an understanding that the wealthy are very different in their attitudes toward their wealth and the legal challenges that having significant wealth brings, you will be in a much better position to effectively communicate with them.

In communicating a tax plan to a Family Steward, for example, you can show how the elements of your proposed legal strategies relate to the wealthy client's goals of using his or her assets to safeguard the family. Detailed technical discussions may be fine, as long as they always link back to the wealthy client's overriding objective of making sure the family is well taken care of.

Communicating a tax plan to a Phobic will be very different. Phobics do not want detailed information. They need to make these difficult decisions without personally going into the details. The best way to help this kind of wealthy client is to work closely with his or her other advisors because a Phobic is reassured when their private client lawyer, their accountant and their wealth manager all agree on a course of action.

Exhibit 10.2 illustrates how high-net-worth personalities differ in their communication needs. By skillfully using a framework like high-net-worth psychology, you can be surer of several outcomes. You can be increasingly assured that your wealthy clients will feel as though their goals, needs and preferences are understood. You will also likely motivate your wealthy clients to act.

**Exhibit 10.2
High-Net-Worth Psychology and Private Client Lawyer Communications**

High-net-worth personality	Needs from private client lawyers
Family Stewards	• Explain how legal strategies will protect family interests • Involve key family members
Phobics	• Work on structuring simple and clear explanations • Work effectively with other trusted advisors
Independents	• Show how legal strategies will foster their goal of personal freedom • Communicate an appreciation of the client's values
Anonymous	• Demonstrate that confidentiality is diligently protected • Communicate respect for their privacy needs
Moguls	• Acknowledge their need for control and power • Show how legal strategies will maintain or increase their ability to influence others
VIPs	• Show an understanding of their need for status and respect • Relate their situation to cases among the "rich and famous"
Accumulators	• Acknowledge their need for wealth accumulation • Relate legal strategies to their need for amassing and protecting capital
Gamblers	• Share nuances of private letter rulings and alternative interpretations of standards • Talk with them about the risks and rewards in alternative legal strategies
Innovators	• Share details of the technical aspects of the recommended legal strategies • Focus on state-of-the-art tax strategies and related products

For the best results, connect your wealthy clients to what is truly important to them. High-net-worth psychology helps you do this. Family Stewards, for instance, are not interested in intentionally defective trusts; they are interested in their families. Phobics are not concerned with the mechanics of tax-wise charitable giving. Instead, they want someone else to take care of the matter for them.

Keep in mind that employing high-net-worth psychology does not change the nature or character of the legal strategies you recommend and provide. It simply allows you to explain these legal strategies in ways that meaningfully resonate with your wealthy clients.

The takeaways

Effectively communicating your legal strategies is critical to building an exceptional high-net-worth legal practice and using the practice as a foundation for potentially building serious wealth. However, it's common for many private client lawyers to do a less-than-excellent job of communicating with their wealthy clients. Effectively communicating by using high-net-worth psychology is a skill that sometimes must be learned and mastered as carefully as the law itself.

Generally a good start is to avoid legalese when speaking with the wealthy and often with their other advisors too. Being able to really connect with your wealthy clients by tying your expertise to their principal motivations will frequently produce outstanding results. One of the best ways to accomplish this is by using high-net-worth psychology.

Delivering the best legal advice and strategies to high-net-worth clients is fundamental to being a high-quality private client lawyer. The ability to do well financially is secondary. Doing well financially requires being appropriately compensated for your expertise, which leads us to value-based project fees.

CHAPTER 11

Profit from Value-Based Project Fees

To create an exceptional high-net-worth legal practice and potentially build serious wealth, you must generate meaningful revenue in return for providing your expertise. Traditionally, private client legal fees are based on the time + expenses model, with many lawyers tracking time in five-, ten- or 15-minute increments.

Most wealthy clients have been exposed to the time + expenses model and to paying top rates for top legal advice. Indeed, many private client lawyers have taken some pains to get their wealthy clients accustomed to this compensation arrangement. However, the wealthy are generally displeased by time + expenses billing and are increasingly becoming disinclined to engage private client lawyers who work solely on this basis.

Alternative fee structures

As customary as time + expenses legal billing may be, the wealthy are becoming progressively critical of that practice, complaining that, in the end, the fees are too high and that billings based on time spent entail an implicit conflict of interest. The general feeling is that private client lawyers who should be working on their behalf are subtly pressured to maximize rather than minimize the time spent.

A major disadvantage to using time-based billing is the approach sets a ceiling for what you can earn. There is only so much you can charge for an hour of time. And as there are only so many hours in a year and there is a high, but limited, ability to leverage junior partners and associates, there is only so much you can bill.

Alternative fee structures can circumvent the dislike many of the wealthy have for time + expenses billing while breaking through the revenue ceiling it imposes on private client lawyers. Specifically, value-based project fees and retainer fees are much more appealing to many of the wealthy. When well thought out, effectively systematized and properly communicated, value-based project fees and retainer fees result in significant revenue increases for private client lawyers.

Core to these alternative compensation arrangements is that they transfer profit generation risk from high-net-worth clients to the private client lawyers. This risk transfer tends to make many private client lawyers anxious and circumspect. Consequently, they choose not to adopt value-based project or retainer fees. For many of them, this might very well be shortsighted.

By adroitly combining alternative fee structures with an intense commitment to effectively communicate legal solutions, the consistent outcome is greater revenue for private client lawyers. These two alternative compensation models provide the opportunity for premium pricing, which translates into substantially greater revenues.

Although time + expenses billing can be less productive than other types of compensation arrangements, it's still the norm among private client lawyers. Overall, slightly more than three-quarters of the private client lawyers surveyed *predominantly* use the time + expenses approach (Exhibit 11.1).

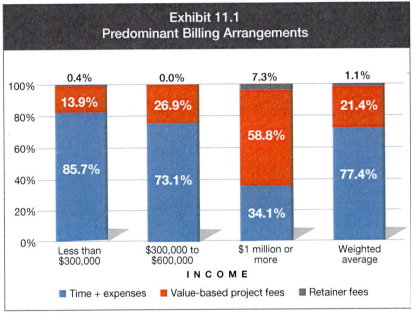

N = 359 private client lawyers. Source: AES Nation.

Only about a fifth of the private client lawyers are using mainly a value-based project fees approach, while very few are employing principally retainer arrangements. However, time + expenses billing is heavily weighted to private client lawyers annually earning $600,000 or less. It's very instructional that more of the elite private client lawyers are using value-based project fees as opposed to time + expenses billing. This is very likely a function of the wealth and consequently the leverage of the high-net-worth clients as evidenced by the preferred approach single-family offices use to pay for private client legal services.

Fee acceptance: a view from single-family offices

In a survey of 199 single-family offices that are all regularly using the services of private client lawyers, about 85 percent of them strongly prefer paying value-based project fees for legal expertise (see Exhibit 11.2). This way, senior management of single-family offices set the parameters for the engagement, including establishing the upper limits on cost. Of course, if the parameters change then the value-based project fees change.

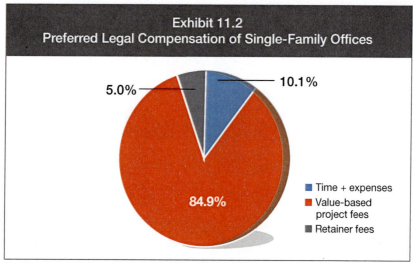

N = 199 senior executives at singly-family offices. Source: AES Nation.

The root of client dissatisfaction with time + expenses billing is usually not the cost of legal services per se, but the cost in relation to the perceived value delivered. Previous research has showed that only a modest percentage of wealthy clients say that their private client lawyers' rates per se are too high. Keep in mind that the wealthy knew the hourly rates when they engaged their private client lawyers; had they felt that the rates were out of line, they could have opted for a less-expensive alternative.

The difficulties do not arise from the hourly rates themselves. They arise when the hourly rates are multiplied by the hours to create the final fee. The consensus is that private client lawyers are charging them for too many hours. This situation is complicated by the fact that the wealthy tend to not have a very good idea of what private client lawyers do or why it takes so long.

Only 5 percent of senior executives at single-family offices prefer retainer fees. This is a function of the general perception that private client lawyers will end up being compensated for not doing that much over time, therefore making value-based project fees a better option.

Paying on a per-project basis certainly lends greater control. Further, a value-based project fee is a familiar arrangement to many successful business owner clients—the preferred type of client of private client lawyers. But as noted, a main reason wealthy clients favor value-based project fees is because *they transfer the profitability risk from the clients to their private client lawyers.*

At first glance, this might seem like bad news for private client lawyers. We have found that in explaining this preference to private client lawyers, the initial reaction among many is that value-based project fees will result in lower revenues than time + expenses compensation arrangements. In actuality, value-based project fees open a set of attractive new possibilities for private client lawyers. Specifically, they enable core compensation metrics, which can then be employed to design value-based fee models leading to higher earnings because of premium pricing—if the private client lawyers effectively communicate the value of the legal services they deliver.

Value-based project fees

For value-based project fees to be the preferred compensation model, there must be an underlying premise: Private client lawyers are not being compensated for their time as much as they are for their expertise and experience. The criterion for being paid well is results achieved, not hours worked. As we have said, this requires private client lawyers to effectively communicate with their wealthy clients. This in turn creates high levels of appreciation for their efforts and a solid belief in the projected outcomes.

High-net-worth clients will pay well for the legal results they seek. This premise has been repeatedly empirically validated. The key point here is that the legal strategies produce the desired outcomes. Wealthy clients have the money and are willing to pay for value so long as they can believe they are, in fact, getting value.

You stand to gain several benefits by using value-based project fees:

- **A matter of expertise.** Value-based project fees can provide appropriate and sometimes disproportionate compensation to you for delivering high-caliber expertise. The contention is that you should be compensated not for the time you spend on a matter, but for the results you provide your wealthy clients. It is as close to a results-oriented compensation structure as possible when it comes to many types of legal services.

- **Wealthy client-centered.** Because of how they are structured, value-based project fees enable you to focus tightly on delivering legal strategies to your wealthy clients, not on billing. Critically, the fee structure enables you to avoid the bias of spending time inefficiently. It is quite the opposite, in fact, because value-based project fees promote efficiency.

- **Wealthy clients equate certain costs with value.** To charge value-based project fees, you must explain and justify them by effectively communicating with your high-net-worth clients. In creating this basis of shared understanding, value-based project fees easily lead to higher client satisfaction and greater revenues. As we discussed in the previous chapter, high-net-worth psychology can play an instrumental role in communicating the value of your legal strategies, as well as validating the value-based project fee being charged.

- **Prompts action.** Extensive research has shown that with value-based project fees, wealthy clients are more positively disposed to implement their private client lawyer's recommendations. Because a percentage of high-net-worth clients choose not to implement the recommendations of their private client lawyers, with value-based project fees, more wealthy clients will likely follow through.

When using value-based project fees, you must clearly communicate the benefits to your wealthy clients in advance. This communication should include a checklist of defined activities that you will undertake, along with a list of the deliverables and results you will provide. Moreover, by using high-net-worth psychology, you are better able to imbue your legal strategies with significance and usefulness as perceived by your wealthy clients.

The value-based, project-based approach represents a change from the traditional time + expense compensation model. And while the case for making the transition to value-based project fees is compelling, many private client lawyers—even those who dislike the time + expenses model—are understandably cautious. For wealthy clients and private client lawyers alike, there are two major misconceptions that may be keeping them from seeing the benefits of value-based project fees:

- **Failing to understand the cost structure of delivering high-quality legal advice.** To quote a price from the beginning and make money requires a strong understanding of a law practice's cost structure and a clear idea of the talent and resource requirements demanded by the engagement. The key to developing a value-based project fees structure is to think in terms of margins and the bottom line, not the top line—the fees. This is not actually all that difficult. In working with elite private client lawyers on setting value-based project fee structures, we have been consistently able to produce sizable increases in revenues.

- **Failing to translate the benefits of their advice into value for the wealthy client.** Wealthy clients need to understand the value they receive for the fees they are charged. Presently, relatively few private client lawyers understand how to systematically explain the value they are delivering, which is where high-net-worth psychology fits in. Again, in working with private client lawyers, we have helped them better frame their expertise using high-net-worth psychology, resulting in little to no pushback on pricing.

Value-based project fees are not about costs and hours of effort. They are about outputs and benefits. Benefits and outputs are the results of the legal advice delivered to wealthy clients. Examples include more money retained for heirs or going to charity because of an estate plan, the financial and family benefits of a business succession process, and current savings due to skillful income tax planning.

In positioning value-based project fees to a wealthy client, it's critical to specify the deliverables and benefits. This makes the value you will deliver tangible. Optimally, you will inform your wealthy clients upfront how much they will gain financially and how the proposed legal strategies foster the high-net-worth client's personal and professional agendas.

Constructing value-based project fees

The process for constructing and communicating value-based project fee structures is very well developed. You can apply a variety of different methodologies.

The easiest and, admittedly, the least consistently precise approach is to estimate the number of hours it usually takes to deliver certain expertise, such as producing a charitable remainder trust, and multiply the time by a billing rate for the lawyers involved. Then provide that number—often with some slack—to your wealthy client. As we have been emphasizing, to garner acceptance of the value-based project fee, you would be well-advised to frame the conversation with the benefits that will accrue by using high-net-worth psychology.

This approach requires you to have a good grasp of expected time requirements of providing different legal strategies. It may also be the best place to start to become adept at moving from time + expense billing to value-based project fees.

Once you have experience with value-based project fees, you will develop insights as to what you need to charge for your legal services to make a worthwhile profit. This approach takes informed guesswork refined by critical systematic evaluations of consequences. Techniques such as profitability matrices and deliverables/cost-structure analyses can be quite helpful. It is very important to accurately understand your fully loaded costs, including operational and business development costs.

A more advanced and powerful version of this methodology entails taking the insights you have gained and algorithmically determining the range of value-based project fees for each legal strategy by high-probability wealthy client situation, taking into account verifiable profit margins and all fully loaded costs. With enough information, this approach can be made pretty much mechanical while producing substantial profits and helping you build serious wealth.

The takeaways

High-net-worth clients, by and large, do not like the time + expenses compensation system currently employed by most private client lawyers. They may resent the bills they receive and sometimes distrust the advice they get to the extent that they will not implement their private client lawyers' recommendations. They may feel that their private client lawyers do not understand them or what they are trying to achieve.

As a result, many private client lawyers see their compensation levels falling. Slowly, win-win solutions are emerging. Value-based project fees can amply reward you as you provide high-quality legal strategies to your wealthy clients. There is no question that value-based project fees have considerable promise for high-net-worth clients and their private client lawyers.

EXCELLING IN TURBULENT TIMES

In the previous chapters, we set out five best practices that can help you build an exceptional high-net-worth legal practice and set the stage for serious wealth. These are not the only best practices, but to get moving quickly, they are the ones most likely to help you navigate a very challenging environment and create an exceptional high-net-worth legal practice.

From here, it is very possible to become seriously wealthy. We'll conclude by taking another look at what it takes to build significant wealth.

EXCELLING IN TURBULENT TIMES

CONCLUSION
Building Great Wealth Revisited

Looking across the profession, very few private client lawyers are presently on track to become seriously wealthy or even to become substantially wealthier. In fact, a considerable number are more likely to see their incomes and wealth diminish than rise. This is the stark reality in spite of the fact that most private client lawyers say they really want to be wealthier than they are today.

Coping in an uncertain environment

The nature of most high-net-worth legal practices is not necessarily geared to enable lawyers to earn truly significant sums or amass substantial private fortunes. As we've discussed, in many situations, this is structural—a function of earning capacity and the nature of the legal profession (for example, time + expenses billing and leveraging junior professionals).

Further complicating the matter is the fact that the great majority of private client lawyers believe they are working in a turbulent business environment that is only likely to become more difficult, adversely impacting their ability to be successful. There are many well-founded reasons for this perception:

- Private client lawyers tend to see more competition from other lawyers as well as strong and growing competition from non-lawyers.

- Legal services are more and more becoming commoditized (although there are still ways to ensure differentiation).

- There is an ever-present possibility of major adverse changes in tax law and planning strategies, which can reduce the opportunities for private client lawyers to provide their services.

- High-net-worth clients are becoming more and more cost-sensitive. This is putting downward pressure on fees, especially for those private client lawyers using the time + expenses approach to billing.

- The growing challenges in sourcing wealthy clients can be overcome by the skillful use of methodologies such as street-smart networking and actions to become thought leaders, but not many private client lawyers are adept at employing these processes.

All these factors combine to drive down the earnings power, the incomes and the wealth of private client lawyers.

While the legal environment is changing in many pronounced respects and not always for the better, this does not negate the fact that you can still earn a very good living. The demand for your expertise remains high and is even expanding as high-net-worth families increase in number along with the amount of wealth they control. Still, there is often a wide gulf between a very good living and building serious wealth.

Putting yourself in the line of money

We want to be crystal clear: By concentrating on high-potential, high-net-worth clients, you can most probably step up your earning capacity and thus your income in a huge way. There are several types of high-net-worth clients who will likely enable you to generate comparatively disproportionate revenue.

For most private client lawyers, the optimal high-net-worth clients are successful business owners. They have needs and wants you can address, and because of their business interests, you can provide many other types of legal services to them and their companies by bringing in other lawyers. This combination of delivering legal strategies to the wealthy family along with the firm can translate into considerable revenue. If your high-net-worth legal practice is well-managed, significant money will flow to the bottom line and into your pocket.

For a much smaller number of extraordinarily capable private client lawyers, the Super Rich and single-family offices prove to be incredibly worthwhile high-net-worth clients. Single-family offices usually require a panoply of legal services that a clever, competent private client lawyer can deliver. Not surprisingly, these two often-interrelated types of high-net-worth clients can generate astounding revenues for private client lawyers because of their ongoing and diverse legal needs and wants.

Other types of high-net-worth clients include fine art collectors, corporate executives, inheritors and celebrities. Also, with so much private wealth being created globally, a multitude of opportunities arise for private client lawyers to deliver legal expertise to multi-territorial clients.

You have additional opportunities to generate considerable revenue. If you can facilitate Super Rich Solutions, that can prove very advantageous. Wealth management products such as private placement life insurance and captive insurance companies provide you with meaningful planning opportunities for wealthy clients. Also, by working cooperatively with high-caliber wealth managers, you may be referred to new wealthy clients. Moreover, because of the nature of these two wealth management products, premium priced retainer fees are very possible. And retainer fees are also possible with other wealth management products.

Another specialty niche is helping wealthy families better cope with their great fortunes. This requires a combination of technical expertise and skilled relationship management. And while many different types of professionals can help ultra-wealthy families deal with this, private client lawyers are regularly tapped to be of assistance.

Implementing best practices

To become seriously wealthy, however, focusing on high-potential, high-net-worth clients and services is just the first step. You will also need to staunchly embrace and skillfully implement the best practices we have discussed.

At the top of the list of best practices is being able to source new wealthy clients. Although client referrals and direct outreach to potential clients can be effective, the most powerful way is usually through referrals from noncompeting professionals. Street-smart networking can be very effective in enabling you to build strategic partnerships with noncompeting professionals while economic glue can drive the success of those partnerships over time.

Being a thought leader can also be very useful in accessing the wealthy on preferential terms. When you are recognized as a thought leader, you are better able to create strategic partnerships and garner more referrals from wealthy clients. Being seen as a thought leader often confers additional benefits such as a shorter sales cycle and stronger relationships with existing high-net-worth clients. Without question, the ability to develop and communicate innovative and meaningful thought leadership content to the wealthy and referral sources can be very useful in building an exceptional high-net-worth legal practice.

Because of the effort usually required to source a new, quality, wealthy client, it makes sense to maximize the relationship, which means providing additional private-client and other types of legal expertise. To make this happen, you must be proactive in generating new opportunities for legal services with your current high-net-worth clients. There are various ways to accomplish this, but using the Total Client Model to create client-centered business development plans has consistently proven to be extremely valuable.

A challenge for some private client lawyers in working with the wealthy is communicating legal strategies as effectively as possible. Some private client lawyers commonly get wrapped up in their own expertise and ingenuity, which can befuddle the wealthy or anyone who is not well-versed in legalese or tax strategies. The consequences can be severe. The wealthy can easily decide to not implement the hard work provided by private client lawyers. Potentially more problematic is when high-net-worth clients proclaim their experience and views to others about the substandard private client lawyers they engaged. There is a very good solution to this challenge: Frame your legal strategies using high-net-worth psychology. Doing so will enable you to productively motivate your wealthy clients and has been shown to foster client referrals.

The traditional time + expenses billing model, while central to many private client lawyers, can be inadequate or even counterproductive when working with the wealthy. It is rarely the hourly rate that evokes criticism, but the number of hours charged. A much preferable approach is value-based project fees. Key to the appeal of value-based project fees is that they shift the economic risk from the wealthy to private client lawyers. For a well-managed high-net-worth legal practice, this billing model may not only suit your wealthy clients, but also can be more profitable for you.

Other factors come into play if you wish to become seriously wealthy. Implementing the best practices we discussed takes real effort. You also need perseverance, as things rarely go smoothly in building an exceptional high-net-worth legal practice. Moreover, perseverance has consistently been shown to be an essential quality of people who have become seriously wealthy because of their own efforts.

Take the steps needed to maximize your personal wealth. This often entails taking chips off the table and benefiting from your own expertise as well as the skills and knowledge of high-caliber wealth managers.

As exemplified by successful business owners, making use of the wealth management services and products regularly used by the Super Rich, single-family offices and ultra-wealthy business owners can help you increase and protect your hard-earned wealth. Many of these wealth management services and products—which we call Super Rich Solutions—can do the same job for you, thereby helping you progress along the path to serious wealth.

Excelling in turbulent times: the takeaways

We've covered a lot of ground here. As you move forward in building an exceptional high-net-worth practice, keep these key points ever at the forefront:

Put yourself in the line of money by serving high-net-worth clients. To become seriously wealthy, you must focus on the right clients and the optimal opportunities:

- The best type of high-net-worth client for most private client lawyers is successful business owners.

- The Super Rich and single-family offices also offer tremendous opportunities, albeit for smaller numbers of private client lawyers.

- A range of other types of high-net-worth clients, including fine art collectors, corporate executives, inheritors, celebrities and multi-territorial clients offer many opportunities.

- Facilitating the delivery of Super Rich Solutions has the potential to generate significant revenue along with referrals to new wealthy clients.

- Helping high-net-worth families cope with the challenges of their wealth is another specialty niche that presents significant opportunities to private client lawyers.

Implement proven best practices. There are five best practices critical to building an exceptional high-net-worth legal practice:

- Source the best high-net-worth clients from noncompeting professionals. Street-smart networking can effectively set the stage for profitable strategic partnerships.

- Benefit from being a thought leader. Expertise is not enough—you also must have intellectual capital to share.

- Maximize your high-net-worth client relationships. This means providing additional private client services as well as bringing in other lawyers to provide other types of legal expertise.

- Communicate your legal strategies effectively. Your use of high-net-worth psychology will be invaluable here.

- Profit from value-based project fees. Your wealthy clients are likely to prefer them to the traditional time + expenses model, and you can potentially realize higher profits.

The next step is yours

It can be challenging for private wealth lawyers to become seriously wealthy, but you absolutely can achieve this financial goal. Very telling, when we have coached and consulted with motivated, talented private client lawyers concerning how to effectively implement the best practices we have discussed, they have been able to considerably increase their revenue, incomes and net worth.

The perspectives and methodologies we have presented here can be transformational for your high-net-worth legal practice. When these best practices are put to work, even at relatively low levels, your earnings can increase—sometimes exponentially. We wish you the best of success on your journey to create an exceptional high-net-worth legal practice and astutely apply Super Rich Solutions to become seriously wealthy.

Made in the USA
San Bernardino, CA
25 July 2017